What I Know about Jumping

Real life lessons on finding the courage to make major life changes—also known as 'jumping off a cliff'—and how my grandmother's secret-coded messages rescued me after jumping

Marcie L. Boyer

Disclaimer

This book is intended to provide support, encouragement, and motivation to those seeking to make major life changes, and is solely the opinion of the author. Many of the stories and examples are based on the author's own life experiences and are true to the best of her ability to remember those events. Other examples are made up and are used in a fictitious manner in order to help illustrate concepts presented in the book. Any resemblance to actual persons—living or dead—or actual events is purely coincidental.

This book is not intended to be a substitute for seeking a diagnosis or treatment for psychological or medical ailments, or for professional advice.

The author has made every attempt to ensure the correctness of the information, and makes no representations or warranties. The author assumes no liability of any kind, whether direct, indirect, or accidental, including psychological, physical, emotional, financial, or commercial loss or damages resulting from the application of information provided within this book.

Published by Marcie L. Boyer
Copyright © 2015 by Marcie L. Boyer
Cover Design by Dennis Champlain, Worthy Image LLC
Editing and formatting by Christine Rice Publishing Services
Digital ISBN: 978-0-9931868-3-7
Trade Paper ISBN: 978-0-9931868-5-1
www.MarcieLBoyer.com

Dear Helen

Wish you all the best on your next jump!

Enjoy!!

Marcie x

Contents

FOREWORD

I believe in the power of story to entertain, instruct, connect, and, ultimately, heal. In fact, I believe that telling one's story can literally save one's life.

So when Marcie Boyer told me that she was finally going to tell her story, I was beyond ecstatic. And when she asked me to write this foreword, well, "humbly honored" is just a start at describing how I felt.

I've known Marcie for about ten years. One of our most powerful conversations happened one day in 2009, when I stopped in to see her at her fair trade store (which you will learn more about in this book) here in New London, CT. We got to chatting.

At the time, I was blogging and also freelancing for *The Day Publishing Company*'s "Grace Magazine." I knew a little bit about Marcie and thought she'd be a great candidate for Grace's "cover girl."

That's when Marcie told me that she did, indeed, have a story to tell, but that she wasn't ready to tell it publicly. When she told me her story, the part of me that loved telling other women's stories was sorely disappointed, but the part of me that knows how important and powerful it is to tell your own story, understood, because it's not mine to tell—it's hers. And she does it so well, in her own truly unique voice. And what a story it is!

"What I Know about Jumping" is part memoir, part day-in-the-life, part workbook. There is no doubt that for Marcie, writing this book was a labor of love.

For you, I hope reading it will be as well.

This book is only the beginning. We are lucky that Marcie has more than this one story in her.

Stay tuned…you are about to experience a powerful voice!

Karen C.L. Anderson

Champion of late bloomers and resilient daughters, author, and blogger

In Memory of Rita Mae Durkin (1928 – 1993)

Always a beacon of light in the darkness

Forever my fiercest protector

CHAPTER 1

MY BACKSTORY

What Do I Know about Jumping?

I have always known that I am an abortion-survivor. It has been both a burden and a blessing, sometimes manifesting as an unbearable guilt for surviving when others have not, leading me to believe that I'm not doing enough with the life I've been given. Other times, it has been a loving reminder, motivating me into action when I've been afraid or struggled to find courage. All times, however, it has propelled me into making major life changes—some risky and potentially harmful, others painful yet necessary and life-affirming because of purpose.

Likewise, the fear that drove my Grandmother Rita to pressure my mother into having an illegal abortion in 1969, primarily because of my race, having a white mother and black father, was a result of her love and desire to protect her family from abuse, poverty, and the hate of a world that was not ready to accept mixed-race children. When the abortion failed, and my mother continued to be pregnant, that same fear was transmuted into the deepest love imaginable for me. Aware of the challenges I'd face, my grandmother became my fiercest protector until her last breath. For that, I am eternally grateful.

Being a mixed-race abortion-survivor who grew up in the 1970s *ghetto*, does not define who I am, but it certainly has shaped the person I have become. As much as I want to believe that I'm consciously creating a life based on purpose, that purpose has been molded out of the belief that I'm not supposed to be here—and wasting this opportunity to live has never been an option. While fate would have it that my life's single greatest achievement happened before I was born, and took no act of faith, effort, or courage on my part, it has, however, taken me over forty years to find the courage to accept and, eventually, own it.

Growing up in a big, culturally rich family, I flitted between *Superfly*, *All in the Family*, *The Waltons*, *The Jeffersons*, and *Good Times* on TV and in real life. It goes without saying that my family is the single most influential factor in forming my thinking. Raised in an Irish-Catholic home during the Great Depression, my Grandmother Rita, who this book is based on, came from a small coalmining town in central Pennsylvania. Although she took the lead in raising me, she was supported by a cast of unlikely characters, all of whom were perfectly imperfect.

My White-Irish-French unwed teenage mother, ever fearful that 'something bad' was going to happen to me, smothered me with sickly-sweet love, while drowning her sorrows in a bottle. Now, twenty years sober, she has succumbed to debilitating disabilities. My Northern-Black-Native American-Irish biological father, whose refusal to share his life with me, thankfully did not extend to his accepting middle-class family. His mother loved me as one of her own, instilling pride for my culture, love of music, and deep familial roots. My Southern-Black step-father, my mother's first husband, who, raised me as his own daughter and whom I consider to be my "father," grew up amongst cotton plantations north of Jackson, Mississippi in the 1950s, worked tirelessly to save me in more ways than I can count, but sadly wasn't always able to save himself from using, dealing, and stealing. Last but not least is my mother's second husband, my White-country boy-in-disguise, nearly seven-foot tall, Black step-father, who was my mother's high school friend, former bartender, and drinking partner. In his twenty years of sobriety, he has given me and my daughter tall patriarchal shoulders to stand on.

Although I left home filled with hope for a better life in New York City with my ex-husband, then boyfriend, at the age of nineteen, when I took my first jump, the complex tapestry my family and upbringing had given me never left me. Like a second skin, I initially wore it with shame. Lacking confidence to own the life that I was given, and desperately seeking to live a 'normal' one, I shed the outward appearance of my former life. With maturity, however, my background has given me a foundation to accept differences, seek understanding, and live with purpose and intention, thus honoring my family and the miraculous life I have received. Now living the "forth version" of my life—what I call "Me 4.0"—where, after each jump, one's life is so significantly different that there is little resemblance to the previous life that it becomes a new version, I may not, can not, and will not hide behind my story, the invisible scars it has created, or the guilt for surviving when those before me had not. Nor will I continue to deny the unique insight my life has afforded me.

What I Know about Jumping is my first attempt to convey these insights through the written word. It is about finding the courage to consciously make major life changes—when we want to, when we need to, or when we have no other choice but to. I call this jumping.

Jumping off an imaginary cliff—to be clear, not an actual cliff—is a metaphor for taking a leap of faith. Yes, it requires a great deal of courage to face our deepest fears, but, in return, offers us the opportunity to uncover amazing inner strength that we may never have otherwise known existed. Recognizing we all have a story to live, a path to follow, and cliffs to jump, my hope is that my story may help others searching for the courage to jump!

When I'm not jumping, I can be found exploring markets, visiting new pubs, and settling into a much quieter life in southeast England with (to quote my daughter) my "Neapolitan ice–cream" family: strawberry husband, chocolate daughter, vanilla me, and our middle-aged, dark-fudge cat, Missy (lovingly nicknamed "Zen Master").

As I'm not a trained counselor, therapist, or have any other similar qualification, I cannot tell you what is best for you or advise you on what you should do. My only desire is to share my learnings, thoughts, and ideas. Take what works for you, leave what doesn't, and, if needed, please seek professional help.

CHAPTER 2

MY LAST JUMP

I was set free because my greatest fear had been realized,
And I still had a daughter who I adored,
And I had an old typewriter and a big idea.
And so rock bottom became a solid foundation on which I rebuilt my
life.

J.K. Rowling

This last jump nearly destroyed me. I expected it to be difficult; it was, after all, my third major jump. I thought I was better prepared. It wasn't supposed to be this *hard*. We'd planned for it for three years and considered our options, but none of it softened the blow. Four weeks after the jump, mistakenly believing that I'd landed safely on solid ground, the bottom fell out and I began to free-fall. When I eventually hit the real bottom, it shattered me into a thousand tiny pieces. Everything that was before—gone! I was so broken, I thought I'd never recover. Had I made a mistake? How could I be so terribly, *terribly* wrong?

How it all Started

We agreed one day that we would move to England. That day would come fifteen years later. When we met, my now husband and I each worked on either side of the Atlantic Ocean—otherwise known as "the pond"—for the pharmaceutical giant *Pfizer*. He was a dashing, British, Senior Director living in the United Kingdom, and I was a young, American, Assistant Information Scientist living in the United States. He was White, older, and a scientific doctor. I was Black, young, recently separated, and broke (again). Meeting at a business conference, we formed one of the most unlikely pairs.

Our budding relationship was not only challenged by our vast life and geographical differences, but it was also dependent on his work travel schedule. Therefore, neither of us knew if "We" would make it until his next monthly visit to the States. Five years later, our hopelessly romantic whirlwind relationship between two countries was threatened when my husband, then partner, was offered an early retirement. This left us with two choices: end our relationship or one of us move to the other's country.

Because of our strong commitment to our children, neither option seemed to be a viable one, so we agreed to take the middle road. We decided to build a life together in the States so that my daughter would not be uprooted, and my partner would travel between two homes, dividing his time with us in the States and his adult children in England. Then, when my daughter was "old enough," we would move to my partner's home in England and, if needed, reverse roles: I would fly to the States to visit my daughter. At the time, it *seemed* like the "right" thing to do.

I say *seemed*, because I no longer believe in right or wrong. From a future perspective, right and wrong can be like an old pair of shoes that still fit and look good when worn, but somehow don't feel like "you" anymore. They do not fit the "you" who you are today. They have become irrelevant. Because our views of what is "right" and "wrong" can change with time and are based on our circumstances, similar to our taste for old shoes, the notion of "right" and "wrong," therefore, does not exist. Now living on the other side of a dream, the one thing I know for certain is not what's right or wrong, not what's good or bad, but that there is absolutely nothing I know for certain.

Before the 2008 Recession
Bull by the Ho'

Once we took the middle road, the fc
be divided into two equal parts: *before*
recession. *Before* the recession, life was like a ta.._
with hope, optimism, and big ideas. Money was plentn.._,
I continued working for Pfizer after my partner's retirement.
We bought a spacious home in downtown Mystic,
Connecticut and two brand new cars, landscaped the garden,
traveled to the Caribbean in Februarys, spent annual family
holidays in England, and squeezed in annual adventure
holidays to exotic places, such as Ecuador, India, and Ghana.

This period could be described as expansive. Not expansive
in a glamorous way, as we lived sustainably and traveled
responsibly, balancing our own needs with the needs of
others. It was our thinking and thirst that was expansive. It
was larger than life.

We developed a mantra to describe how we viewed our lives:
"Taking the bull by the horns," which also summed up what
we believed we could accomplish. Building a life purpose
around this mantra, we started a fair trade retail business.
Through the sale of handmade crafts, we expanded others'
views on poverty, and shared the responsibility of helping
others in developing countries. The "We" now had a
mission.

Three years after starting our part-time fair trade business,
and feeling confident in the economic viability of the market,
I left my job at Pfizer to devote myself full-time to our
mission. This allowed me to "make a living, living my
passions." Life was *good*.

the 2008 Recession: The End of a Fairytale

.e many after the 2008 recession, our lives could be .ummed up in one word: *cruel*. The exact date *after* began was announced by George Bush on September 24th 2008: the US was now in a recession. Prior to the announcement, we saw that things were getting tighter, shipping prices were going through the roof, customers were spending more time agonizing over purchases, and growth was slowing. Knee-deep in the retail business, with two employees, $80,000 tied up in inventory, and a 1,700 square foot retail store located in what we called "an artistic, historic, downtown district" (but those not wearing rose-tinted spectacles called "depressed"), like most, we too believed it to be a temporary economic blip. The subtle recessionary tides were slowly creeping in, claiming every second or third storefront with it. Trimming fat where we could, we noticed we were working twice as hard for half the money.

With our backs against the wall, we took off our spectacles and went into full fire-fighting mode to save the business and the "We." Our fairytale life was slowly dissolving and was being replaced with unbelievably sore feet that we iced, unrelenting arguments about money, and worry about our health. Now entering my sixth year without health insurance, as pre-existing conditions coupled with high costs made it nearly impossible to afford, the demands of retail were taking their toll on my body. The relentless schedule of maintaining two homes and a retail business, on top of ten years of flying across the pond, left my partner chronically tired.

Seeing the writing on the wall, we began planning our escape to solid ground: our big jump. My partner's house in England was mortgage-free, and his pension was enough to support us. We'd both have healthcare, and college tuition was still affordable, should my daughter go to college in England. But beyond those reasons, most importantly, it was the compassionate thing to do for my loving partner, who'd been living out of suitcases for thirty years. While we did not put a date on the calendar, we did, however, make the decision to move. We slowly began to tie up the loose ends of our existing lives, so when the opportunity presented itself, we'd be ready to jump into a new one.

The Long Path to the Cliff's Edge

Lured by the promise of healthcare and a steady income, I secured a dream job as a government Business Advisor. For eighteen months, I worked seven days a week, managing our fair trade retail business on the weekends, and by day, helping others in nineteen towns grow theirs. Naïvely believing myself to be superwoman, the weight of the pressure was eventually more than I could bear—something would have to give. Finding myself fifty pounds overweight and on the road (again) to diabetes, I developed high blood pressure.

All was not lost though. The dream job allowed us to fulfill some long lost dreams. We refinanced the mortgage, halving our monthly payments, knowing that should any of our plans not materialize, a lower mortgage would give us more options, and also built our dream kitchen. While we were aware that a new kitchen would improve our chances of selling the house, what I was not aware of was how it triggered me to rethink my eating. I started a high-protein diet and lost forty pounds in five months. Losing the weight not only restored my health, but it gave me the strength to let go of more than just my fat. Heartbreakingly, we decided to sell our fair trade business, and with it, our original purpose.

Six months after selling the business, I was unexpectedly laid off, and again with no health insurance. While it was my fifth time uninsured, and knowing I'd been uninsured about half of my adult life, I wasn't too unsettled by this latest turn of events, but as a parent of an uninsured child, it terrified me. And for the first time in my 25-year career, I became not only one of the millions of uninsured Americans, but I was now also unemployed—with no job or business.

Uncertain of how it would all work out, we were not deterred from taking our first definitive steps towards an *unknown* cliff—we still had no assurance that our plans to move would come to fruition—and we continued on the path as planned. Among them was organizing a long overdue wedding in six weeks. After fourteen years of sharing our lives together, I married my life partner and soul mate on a beautiful beach in Jamaica, with parents, kids, and grandkids with us. But with little time to bask in the glow of being newlyweds, we arrived home from Jamaica and continued our journey along the path to the cliff's edge.

Over the next six months, we increased our planning efforts. With a heavy heart, I watched my loved ones suffer. I coerced my daughter into growing up faster than she was emotionally ready, by pressuring her to make a major life decision for herself: whether to attend college in England or the States. While she struggled with her decision and completed college applications, I forced her to study for the entrance exams, sent her to testing tutors, and helped her study—by re-learning high school math myself.

My new husband agonized with worry, losing countless hours of sleep completing our UK visa applications and the Zen Master's pet passport. If all of that wasn't enough on our plates, we began fixing ten years of home repairs that we had been unable to do because of the business, while simultaneously repainting half of the house white, at the suggestion of the home inspector—to appease the "unimaginative" prospective buyers, who would only buy houses with white interior walls.

The thing was, up until two months before our move, we still did not know if we would be moving—that is, if we would be jumping. The final decision was not ours to make. That power was in the hands of the UK Border Agency. While we had made our decision over thirty months prior, and were anxiously making our way to the edge, the reality was, we had no control over the final decision. We were keenly aware of the harsh truth of our reality: when we came to the end of the long path to the cliff's edge, it was possible that there may be no cliff to jump, or it may be a different cliff than the one we'd planned to jump. It was difficult to ignore the fact that we might be forced to return from the supposed cliff's edge and get on with our lives as best as we could—together or apart.

Not until our UK visas arrived did our plans become a reality—only then could we clearly see the end of the road and the cliff's edge. With our visas in hand, we cried tears of relief and tears of sorrow, as life had become unbearable. Having less than ninety days to leave the States, we gave away, donated, and sold three lifetimes of memories as we methodically emptied the contents of our 2,800 square foot home through Craig's List and soul-destroying, vulture-circling yard sales. The few remaining items between the three of us, we packed into twenty banker boxes, four dish cartons, five bags of clothing, and two suitcases each. After saying goodbye to our empty dream home, swimming pool, fish pond, waterfalls, and resident frog, Nelson, we walked away from our dissolving fairytale life and made our way to the cliff's edge.

We Closed our Eyes and JUMPED!

Arriving at Boston's Logan Airport, with excess luggage filled to maximum weight, wearing two sets of clothing, extra sweaters, and hats, and having checked the Zen Master into cargo, my husband, daughter, and I thought the worst was over. While we sat drinking cocktails, saying last tearful goodbyes to our family, we neglected to hear the announcements about the fire at the fueling station. Shortly after going through the security gate, we learned that all of the international flights were canceled! That had *never* happened to us before! In shock, we confirmed Zen Master was deplaned and quarantined to a local veterinary hospital, collected our excess luggage, then exhaustedly boarded buses bound for Hyannis Port, Cape Cod, two hours away—as most of the city's hotels were full and unable to accommodate the sheer volume of stranded international travelers.

The next day was a real-life *Groundhog Day* (minus Bill Murray): same airport, same flight, but a different day. This time, however, after experiencing that painful day twice— saying tearful goodbyes to family, re-checking excess luggage, confirming Zen Master was on the plane—we hoped that we would never, *ever* have to repeat that day again.

Upon arriving in the *Old Country*, all of our focus shifted to getting my daughter to college (university, or uni for short). Now shortened by one day, due to the cancelled flight, we had only six days to unpack, replace discarded items previously owned on the other side of the pond, and repack my daughter's bags for uni.

Mistakenly thinking we'd left the ominous "bad penny" on the rescheduled plane, we celebrated my daughter's 18th birthday under the threat of a looming US government shutdown, and wished that her student loan would not be affected. Watching in horror as the dollar sunk to a 16-

month low, as a result of the US government shutdown and the political battles being played out in the States, we lost hundreds of pounds needed to pay for my daughter's accommodations.

Six days after our jump, we set out again, this time to take my daughter to uni. During the two-hour car journey, we were bemused when we saw a large black object flying past our packed-to-the-ceiling car, and soon realized it was a chunk of our tire! Narrowly escaping a major tire blow-out, we made yet another detour, this time to purchase a new tire. After safely arriving at uni, my daughter quickly settled into her room. Thankfully, she was assigned to an international *flat* (room) in the halls, which allowed her to be amongst others who were a long way from home.

A few short weeks after our arrival, with our feet firmly planted at the bottom of the cliff (or so I thought), I looked forward to my first NHS doctor's appointment, also known as "socialized medicine" in the States. It was to no one's surprise—least of all the doctor and nurse who compassionately empathized with the tearful shell of a person sitting in their exam room—when I learned my high blood pressure was back, along with a host of new painful and mysterious ailments.

Freefalling, Finding Bottom, and Rebuilding

Four weeks after arriving in England, with my daughter settled at uni, Zen Master adjusting to the new smells of the house, and my husband and I slowly fighting our way through his fully-stocked house of twenty-six years to create space for our combined lives under one roof, I felt relieved that we had safely landed. Having been to hell and back, I secretly allowed myself to think, *Surely, life would get better now.*

But with all the distractions from the ensuing chaos, I was unable to hear the cracking earth below my feet or feel its unsteadiness. Nor did I see the tiny pebbles falling away from the sides. I woke up one morning and found the ground had simply disappeared beneath me, leaving me to freefall into the darkest depths of despair. Believing myself to be a loving, rational, giving person, and, for the most part, detached from material possessions, I was unprepared for the unimaginable grief that overtook me.

In my infinite wisdom, I failed to rationalize the effect that one life event would have on me, let alone a multitude of events happening all at once: the gut-wrenching pain of an empty nest, laden with guilt for making my daughter go through this with me; moving not just 500 miles away from my disabled mother, as I had at nineteen years old, but adding 3,000 more miles between us, precisely when she needed me the most; leaving friendships that had taken twenty years to build; dealing with the "after-effects" of selling possessions, caused by my refusal to believe that they defined me, but realizing that they really had; donating furniture passed down through generations; throwing away childhood memorabilia; and selling my dream home that few had wanted to buy.

While I'd consciously made those decisions, I did not consciously plan to become an out-of-work immigrant, perpetually looking for a job—and not the much desired expatriate (expat for short)—by giving up the one thing I had sworn never to give up—to both myself and my women ancestors spanning generations, whose "never depend on a man" advice forever echoed in my soul's ear—my financial independence.

An endless well of tears filled me and I simply could not stop crying. After freefalling for what felt like an eternity, I finally hit bottom. Feeling its cold, damp hardness pressed against my face, racked with pain from the impact of landing and barely able to move, all I could see surrounding my 40-something broken body was the splintered shards of what used to be me.

Having already had a lifetime of successful jumps—some painful, some joyful—it became evident that this jump was unlike any other. I could not simply do what I'd done before. I could not pick up the broken pieces of glass and re-glue my former life together. That life was gone. I needed to completely rebuild me, not from shiny shards of glass, delicately arranged into a beautiful mosaic for others to admire (while exquisite, easily broken), but from the earth: filled with substance. This time, I needed to listen to my soul's sculpture, and chisel a new life from rock, so it could withstand the forces of change coming my way.

Ready to Jump?

CHAPTER 3

LET'S TALK ABOUT JUMPING

Recording with Robert Plant was like jumping off a cliff.

Robert and I did it to have fun and see what would happen, but to start with it was very scary because both of us were out of our comfort zones. We were away from our usual environments so we just had to go with what we felt...

Alison Krauss

What is Jumping?

Simply put, jumping is making a life-altering change. It can be characterized by three fundamental elements: making a conscious decision, acting on that decision, and experiencing intense fear. Typically, the potential benefits of jumping outweigh the consequences of not jumping; meaning, we anticipate our lives will be better if we jump than if we do not. We may jump to get out of a negative situation or into a positive one.

No matter the reason for the jump, there is one differentiating factor that sets jumping apart from ordinary everyday decisions, and that is the intense fear we may feel. This fear is primarily created by the magnitude of the decision—or in other words, the amount of changes we think we will be faced with once we jump—and the unknown corresponding risk, as we are unable to fully envision how the changes will impact our lives. It is this intense fear that stops most people from jumping.

There is no way around it: jumping always pushes us out of our comfort zone. If it didn't, it would not be jumping. Jumping is doing something that scares the shit out of us, but we still do it, because we believe life will be better. The decision to jump is largely driven by our internal motivations, perceptions, and fears. As a result, others may not see our situation or our desire to jump in the same way that we do. There will be some who will not agree with our decision to jump; some may even view it as irrational. By its nature, jumping flies in the face of convention, as few find the courage to jump. Along these same lines, when we make a seemingly risky change, it is often referred to metaphorically as "jumping off a cliff."

Why do we need to use a visual to describe jumping? Because *thinking* about jumping is as real to our bodies as actually jumping. If you've ever seen the movie *The Matrix*, you will instantly understand. The thought of jumping may only be in our mind, but our body does not know that. Our body will react to what's going on in our mind.

Therefore, when we think, plan, or begin to act on a difficult life-changing decision, it may actually feel as though we're about to jump off a very real cliff. That's how it felt for me each time that I jumped. Fear crept into every cell of my body, wreaking havoc throughout. As one should expect it to be, it is our biologically hard-wired warning system alerting us to danger, because our bodies know that jumping off a cliff could kill us.

In spite of the fear, there is far more to gain, as jumping takes us on a journey of self-discovery. It requires a great deal of courage, and forces us to come face-to-face with our fears. Most importantly, however, it offers us the opportunity to overcome those fears; hence, the greater the risk, the higher the jump, so the deeper the fears that will come to the surface.

Proof of Concept

The concept of jumping first came to me while I was contemplating leaving my well-paying job at Pfizer to nurture our fledgling fair trade retail business. On one hand, I was making much more money than I needed to survive, and on the other hand, I was doing something that I felt very passionate about. During the day, I worked in an office; at night and on weekends, I traveled to sell at fairs and festivals, and also waited on customers in our store. The office job fed my belly; the retail business fed my soul. After two years of doing both, it became clear to me that continuing with my job—that is, keeping the thing that fed my belly—would eventually destroy my soul.

At that time in late-2005—three years before the recession—life was relatively "good" for most, so I assumed that I was the only one suffering from the stress of a job. In retrospect, what was happening at Pfizer was happening everywhere. Many theorize it was caused by the collapse of the post-war Golden Age. The same story was being played out over and over on the nightly news: corporate mergers, acquisitions, massive layoffs, site closures, relocations, offshoring, and the continual drive to prop up share prices. But what the nightly news wasn't telling us in their 30-second sound bite was the very real human cost of the collapse.

It took me weeks to accept what was happening. While I was in denial, I did not allow myself to seriously consider leaving my job. My partner and I agreed that I would stay at Pfizer until the retail business was earning money to pay me—even just a tiny fraction of—my previous salary. By the end of our second year, the business was growing strong; therefore, it needed more money than it was making.

My partner had been fortunate to take an early retirement before we started the business, so he was financially secure. However, I'd planned to save one year's salary for the proverbial "nest egg" and then drip-feed it back into our household budget over three years. While I always had a plan, I rarely stuck to them, as was also the case here. The persistent niggling thought that my retirement savings could be used as the nest egg only fueled my desire to leave. Increasingly, I was beginning to believe that it was better to invest it into my future, than possibly lose it in the stock market (which would have happened in 2008 had I left it there).

Unaware of the turmoil brewing within, and in agony from intense pains in my back and neck, I was unable to eat or sleep for weeks. Then a series of profound events occurred when I began seeking medical treatment for the pain (apologetically, too long to describe here), which I believed my indecision was causing. As a result, it became very clear to me that I needed to leave my job. I was slowly beginning to accept this realization.

Once I admitted to myself that I needed to leave my job, one night, while drifting off to sleep, for the first time I saw myself standing at the edge of a cliff. Sick with worry, as I am deathly terrified of heights, I realized someone was quietly whispering into my ear: *JUMP!*

It wasn't the first time I'd made a life-changing decision. I'd already made a lifetime of hard decisions by then—way too many for someone so young. They had been easier, because they had been made out of necessity, bored out of expectation, and needed for my own survival.

I'd left the shackles of poverty by committing myself to working hard, taking jobs whenever I could—and as young as I was able—going to college, and paying my own way in the world. As an only child, I tore my mother's heart to pieces by escaping the crazy, abusive, drunken existence she and her husband had inflicted on each other and on me. I turned my back from the pain of watching my "father" struggle with his crack addiction and his increasing stays in jail. I'd left my home and my friends and family, and moved within four states over a five-year period, before I finally settled down to raise a family. Then, heartbreakingly, several years later, I had found myself divorced, with a three-year-old in tow.

This time was *different*. This time wasn't about physical or emotional survival. It wasn't about leaving something bad for something better. It was the reverse. It was about leaving all the things I'd worked so very hard to get: the recognition, the money, the independence; and all the things I was told I was supposed to do: get a good job, make my family proud, be successful. I knew that many mothers from past generations had invested in me, allowing me to get to where I stood. I did not want their life's work, nor their pain and suffering, to be lost on me. So above all else, I had risked losing the security that we—myself and the four generations of mothers in my family—had paid a pound of flesh for, and without it, could possibly hurt my daughter.

For the first time in my 35 years of age, I was terrified to make a decision.

What life-changing decision have you made in your life? How did you feel before and after making the decision? What did you feel once you acted on the decision—in other words, jumped? When was the first time that you feared making a decision? What did you fear the most? Have you ever broken a promise or a commitment, changed plans, or hurt a loved one in order to do something important for yourself? How did it make you feel?

What Stops us from Jumping?

For most of us, it is fear that stops us from jumping. But fear itself is a double-edged sword: It can stop us from jumping, and it can be our greatest source of motivation to jump. One of the biggest challenges we face, however, is recognizing our own fears, as they may be very well-disguised in our everyday life. They can be internally derived, such as the desire to feel loved, the want to be accepted, or the fear of rejection. Or they may be subconsciously derived, deeply hinged upon our beliefs, such as when we feel good or bad, worthy or unworthy. We may find that we are able to see them more clearly when out of our comfort zone—that is, feeling vulnerable and lacking control in our lives. It is safe to assume that we will better understand our fears after landing.

Stemming from my role as a granddaughter, daughter, wife, and especially as a mother, the fear of failure and not living up to other people's expectations are the two fears I have struggled with the most. The fear of disappointing my grandmother, or wanting to be a "good" wife or mother, has stopped me from jumping off the right cliff. And those same fears have also led me to jumping off the wrong cliff.

However, my greatest fear—the one that gets me hook, line, and sinker; that, when push comes to shove, I cannot deny, that I must listen to—is the fear of not living my life's purpose. I am 100% certain that this fear stems from being an abortion-survivor and is a legacy of survivor's guilt.

Whether the fear stems from an internal source or from a deeper subconscious belief, I have decided that the root cause of the fear is no longer relevant, not because it is unimportant—for it is very important—but because I have decided that the process of overcoming my fear is *more* important.

As we grow up, develop into adults, reach maturity, and accept that our lives will end, it is inevitable that we will face new challenges. Likewise, our fears will evolve, change, and morph, in order to adjust to our new stage of life. Fear is a natural part of living. Consciously embracing my fears has given me the opportunity and the motivation to live life to the fullest—*my* fullest, not other people's definition of fullest.

The bottom line is: fear can weigh us down and keep us from experiencing joy. It can make us feel downright awful, and because of this, we may find that we emotionally dislike feeling fear. Do not be mistaken, however; just because we dislike it, or even hate feeling it, that alone will not make us braver or give us courage, no matter how strong a dislike we have for fear. In fact, it may have the opposite effect; meaning, the dislike may actually contribute to us feeling more fearful—unless we consciously choose to change this dynamic. I have created analogies to help me cope with the emotional aspect of facing my fears.

My Other Best Friend

I'm thoroughly convinced that I'm one of the biggest "courageous" cowards there is. I'd love to take the easy way through life, happily avoiding situations that push me out of my comfort zone, as deep inside I am a coward. But my soul will not allow it, because, for me, it always comes back to purpose, which is more important to me than the uncomfortable feeling of vulnerability. Until I am able to effectively talk my soul into ignoring my purpose and allowing me to be the coward I truly want to be, I have had to find a rational, non-emotional way of dealing with my fears.

This has led me to think of my fears as my "other" best friend. One of my longest best friends, Rhonda, is a force to be reckoned with. She knows me better than most and can tell me things that no one else can—things I am unable to, or do not want to, see about myself. She tells me like it is—no sugar-coating, and not how I'd like it to be (the impact is usually softened with a few glasses of wine). And while I often disagree with her (who wants to hear difficult things about themselves?), I cannot lie: I begrudgingly listen to her (but please don't tell her!).

For her honesty with me, I love her dearly. Fear does the same thing. It brings up issues we are unable to, or choose not to, see, and gives us the opportunity to overcome them—much like a loving best friend. Sadly, sometimes both of them—fear and the people we love—gang up on us, as they recently have with my fear of driving.

Before moving to England, I'd been an avid driver for twenty-seven years. My friends and family can attest that I am a safe, confident driver, having had only one accident (in Boston). In a way, that kind of doesn't count; if you've ever driven in Boston, you'll probably agree. My first car was a 1977 Mercury Cougar, which my Grandmother Rita bought for me when I was sixteen years old so that I could get home from my housekeeping job, as my shift ended after the last bus. However, only being a hair over five feet tall, I was unable to see over the steering wheel without the use of an assortment of pillows on the bench seat, which forced taller folks to sit with their knees to their chests, or sit in the back. From driving gas-guzzling boats, like my Cougar, to small, efficient cars and pickup trucks, I've never shied away from driving, even growing up in the US snow capital: Erie, Pennsylvania. That all changed when I moved to England.

Shortly before our move, my husband bought a fairly new BMW from a friend, who could no longer drive due to health reasons. The car was sleek, sophisticated, and was what it said it was: the ultimate driving machine. When I first began driving it, I broke out in a sweaty panic attack. For starters, I had difficulty seeing over the dashboard. And the physical sensation of seeing cars zooming past on my right side sent my nerves into overload. Many times, I'd break down into tears just sitting behind the steering wheel. The thought of driving was more than I could bear. My husband and I began to have major fights, because I flat-out refused to drive. Over time, I gradually began driving on motorways, rather than the small, winding village roads, which have always been a source of my anxiety—even as a passenger.

Several months after moving, I spoke with Rhonda and explained to her that I was still not driving, except on the rare motorway trip. I told her that, while I disliked the loss of my independence, when my husband couldn't drive me, or when I wanted to flex my wings, I caught buses and trains. While I preferred public transportation, unfortunately, in Southeast Kent, it wasn't practical.

I told her how I couldn't see properly, the drivers were more aggressive, there was little room on the "roads," I constantly had to weave in and out of parked cars, I sometimes had to reverse out to let another car pass…my list was endless. She listened patiently for me to finish my long list of excuses, then responded without a hint of hesitation.

"You're afraid to scratch the car, aren't you?" she said.

"No," I said in a semi-automatic defense. "That's not it…*really*. I can't see, and they drive crazy here," I pleaded.

Silence.

"You're afraid to scratch the car, aren't you?" she said again, to make sure I had heard her.

"Alright, alright…if you put it like that, no, I don't wanna scratch the car, but that's not it really," half-acquiescing to her demand.

"You're afraid that David will be mad if you scratch the car?" she dove deeper.

Silence, as I had no further excuses left in my arsenal to defend myself.

"Scratch the fucking car! Just scratch it! Get it out of the way so you can drive! Will you? You got the money to fix it. You'll be keeping somebody employed and you'll get over your fear! This isn't like you, Marcie."

Silence.

"Please just scratch the fucking car."

It would be another six months after she told me to scratch the car—or in other words: jump—before I began to take my driving lessons seriously. In fact, her "truth-telling" had the opposite effect. I began driving less, since I had become aware of this new fear that I wasn't aware that I had: my fear of scratching the car. While that fear stopped me from continuing my lessons, it wasn't the primary reason why I wasn't driving. The fear needed more time to work its way to the surface; it was much deeper and was connected to the source of my anxiety and panic attacks. I would not understand that fear until I found the courage to get up after landing.

What Do We Need in Order to Jump?

There are few certainties in life—notable exceptions are death and taxes. But I'd like to add "change"! To live, we must change, and there is no uncertainty in that. Life is not constant. We can neither stay in the same place, do the same things, nor live each day as the day before. Life demands change. It requires us to do something different in order to adapt to our ever-changing environment.

Each day we are faced with internal and external changes, within and without our control. Today, you may be feeling well, on top of the world. Tomorrow, you come down with the flu, and it always seems to happen one week before your vacation, leaving you feeling sorry for yourself because you're always sick on your vacation. Today, you have a job you absolutely love at a local elementary school. Without warning, you learn the school is closing and integrating the students into nearby schools. You will be laid off at the end of the school year. On the surface, these changes impact our jobs, our health, and our overall wellbeing. On a deeper level, they can strip us of our ability to support our family, our sense of security, our confidence, and more fundamentally, our belief in ourselves.

If we know this already—that change is the very essence of life—why do we fear it so much? Why do we allow fear of the unknown to hinder our ability to make decisions, follow through with making changes, and deprive us of living the life that we want? What do we need to have in order to facilitate and embrace change for ourselves?

The Role of Confidence and Belief

Like my "best friend" analogy, the way I view the relationship between our confidence and our beliefs is similar to an "old married couple." Like a recently married couple, our confidence and beliefs may start out distinctly different and independent of one another. Similar to how a long-term married couple over time may begin to take on each other's physical characteristics, and increasingly rely on each other, our confidence and beliefs may too begin to "look" alike and grow dependent on each other.

We may have or not have self-confidence, depending on how we feel about our ability to be successful when completing a task or doing an activity. Practically speaking, self-confidence is that little voice in the background that tells us: "Yes, you can do this! You have what it takes to make it work. You know you are a winner," or: "No, you can't do that. Don't even think about trying to do that. You know you're gonna fail."

The important thing to remember is: Confidence can change. Our confidence can waver as a result of many factors. Two common factors that affect our confidence are: when others do not agree with our beliefs, and when we are out of our comfort zone. Having others validate our assessments increases our confidence, as it must be "true" if others believe it is "true." When we are in our comfort zone, we may feel confident that we will succeed; when we are not, we may think we will not be successful. Hence, our level of confidence may heavily influence our ability to make conscious decisions.

Our beliefs, on the other hand, are much deeper than just how we feel about a situation or in ourselves. Beliefs are intrinsic to who we are as a person. Among other things, beliefs are shaped by our values and judgments, our sense of purpose, how we view the meaning of our lives, and the things we are passionate about. In other words, beliefs make us who we are.

To show the difference between confidence and beliefs, take for example an encouraging comment from a teacher. A positive comment from your teacher about your ability to do well may give you the confidence you need to get an "A" on a paper. However, if you believe that getting an "A" will not help you achieve your goals, then you may not put the effort or energy into getting an "A." This is because confidence can be more easily swayed by external influences, while our beliefs cannot.

Our beliefs are internally driven stories that we tell ourselves about ourselves and how we relate to the world: how we view ourselves in the big picture, what is our purpose in life, what are our guiding principles, how we view the actions of others, what our judgments are on what we believe to be right or wrong (or good or bad), how we view our own successes and failures. Additionally: if we view our success as an occasional thing that happens for no apparent reason or we always expect ourselves to be a success, if we view our failures as opportunities or as threats, and if we think our failures make us stronger or they perpetuate the belief that we always fail. Needless to say, our beliefs are much harder to influence than confidence.

Confidence and beliefs are connected over time, similar to that proverbial "old married couple." While confidence may be a short-term, situational thought or feeling, if we keep having those same thoughts or feelings, we are essentially writing a script in our belief system.

Another way to look at it is, every time we tell ourselves that this will or will not happen (or we will or will not be successful), and we get the result we expected, over time we create a powerful story in our brains that we tell ourselves each time we are faced with a situation or attempt to do something.

Suspending judgment for a moment, this is neither a good nor a bad thing; it is simply the way we operate as humans. It is as though each of us has our own internal iTunes library of Mp3 scripts that we associate with ourselves. It's like having a different playlist for work, home, hanging out with friends, etc. Some scripts are listed under the "Recently Added" section, with only a few plays, while others are in the "Top 25 Most Played." The more often we play a script, the stronger the belief becomes.

The "good" thing about this is, we have the power to change our beliefs. By re-writing the scripts that we tell ourselves, over time we may develop a completely new life story. We can re-write our scripts so that they are positive, life-affirming, and support our sense of purpose. Yes, it is that simple.

Are there activities that challenge your confidence? How many times have you given up because you lacked confidence? Can you re-write the script so that you are successful, regardless of the expected outcome? What can you do to keep those positive scripts alive?

Although our confidence and beliefs play a significant role in determining how we think and feel about making changes in our lives, they do not tell the whole story. They set the backdrop. In other words, they create the stage for our responses. By themselves, however, they do not have the final say. Hope and courage do.

The Role of Hope and Courage

Hope and courage are the facilitators for action. Hope is a desire or a wish for a positive outcome, while courage is the ability to make something happen in the face of fear. If we believe our lives will get better, we have hope. Acting on that hope, by taking action to make our lives better, we have courage. Like confidence and beliefs, hope and courage are intertwined, and we create scripts about them in our belief systems as well.

Unlike confidence and beliefs, hope and courage are not dependent on each other, but they can support one another. With hope, we may find courage, and with courage, we may have hope.

Courage may ask us to do what we would not ordinarily do, or what we think we are not capable of doing, when we have hope. It may require us to do something that scares the shit out of us, because we are hopeful that life will be better if we do it. On the other end of the spectrum, courage may ask us, "What is the worst thing that can happen to me, and can I live with it?"

While hope and courage are clearly connected, they have a subtle, yet major, difference between them. It is easier to illustrate this difference by asking the following question: *How does hope encourage us to have courage?* The answer to this question lies deep within our belief system. Another way to ask the question is: *Who do I believe is ultimately responsible for making changes in my life?* Alternatively: *Am I the driver in my life or the passenger?*

In the scripts that we tell ourselves—our life stories—who is the lead actor? Is it you? Or is it someone else? Do you believe that you are responsible for making change happen in your life?

Do you ever think to yourself: *I believe I am responsible for making a change in my life*, but your actions may say otherwise? In my mind, I tell myself that I should change, but I can't. So I wait for someone else to make the change for me, or for the situation to change without my doing, then I do not have to make the change occur myself. And, if I don't like the outcome of the change, I can always blame someone or something else for it.

How our Confidence, Beliefs, Hope, and Courage are Interconnected

Generally speaking, our views about confidence, beliefs, hope, and courage are formed in childhood. As a young child, I helplessly watched my mother struggle to live each day, only finding solace in her twenty-year addiction to alcohol. Often feeling responsible for her, I watched her confidence waver day-to-day, usually believing herself unworthy, and because of her deep-rooted beliefs, she was unable to stop drinking. At times, darkness totally consumed her, leaving her without hope or the courage to live.

After a major car accident, she was forced to stop drinking and has been sober for over twenty years. While she did not actively make the decision to stop drinking, she did make an active decision not to return to drinking, despite having more of a "reason" to drink: her failing health and constant pain. Today, she is frail and broken, like a tiny sparrow, but she endeavors to live. For that, she is a testament to hope and courage. Through her struggles and suffering, she has taught me valuable life lessons on hope and courage (as well as acceptance and compassion). For that, I am grateful for my mother.

From one day to the next, we are constantly changing. However, the rate of change is not constant. Changes may happen slowly, like a slow, intermittent drip: a drink after work on hump day, then a drink after work during Friday's happy hour, then a drink after an argument with a boss... Or it can happen in the blink of an eye, as was the case when my mother crushed three spinal vertebrae in a car accident, three blocks from my dying grandmother's house—a solemn reminder that we are not in control of all of the changes that happen in our lives.

The slow drip of change may be imperceptible to the eye. On the surface, it may appear insignificant to our day-to-day lives, giving us a false sense of comfort that things will be the same tomorrow. We may forget that we live in an ever-changing world. The rate of change and the magnitude of the change are irrelevant. Over time, a slow, intermittent drip, seemingly insignificant, may have the same effect as big, significant, "blink of the eye" changes. Both may require us to jump.

Make no mistake, life will challenge us, leaving no vulnerable stone unturned in our lives. It may challenge our confidence in a situation, or challenge our belief in our abilities to overcome those challenges. We must stay firm in the belief that, no matter the outcome—win or lose, fail or succeed—we will not lose hope. Hope is the most powerful facilitator for change. However, hope does not guarantee change. At the end of the day, we must truly believe that it is our actions, and how we respond to change, that determines the direction of our lives. Above all else, we must have the courage to act.

The following questions I continually ask myself whenever I am fearful. Perhaps they may help you, as they have helped me to find confidence, belief, hope, and courage.

What areas of my life do I find it difficult to have confidence? Why?

What things, should they happen, frighten me the most? Letting down my spouse? Not living up to my 'parents' expectations? Not getting the promotion I had hoped for? Not having enough money?

Am I more afraid of failure or success?

Am I fearful of achieving my goals?

Do I sabotage my own success? Why?

What is the absolute worst thing that can happen to me? Losing my job? The death of a loved one? What would I do? Would I have the courage to act? Could I live with my actions? Why or Why not?

Crisis in Courage

Unfortunately, in our modern Western world, we are increasingly being stripped of courage and it is being replaced with fear. Little by little, fear is eroding the core of our collective courage as a society. Why is this happening? How does it relate to our fear of making major life changes?

It is such a simple answer that it is almost implausible. In my opinion, I believe that, when we feed smaller irrational fears, over time, we create an environment that breeds larger, more significant fears. Another way to say it is, when we lack courage in smaller, seemingly insignificant areas of our lives, we may not find the courage that we need in more important areas of our lives. As a society, we are creating a crisis in courage.

In my unscientific, unproven theory. I believe this is largely a result of the creation of the consumer culture, which took hold in the late-1950s. Prior to the advancement of technologies, and the rise of consumerism, we faced real dangers every day, and in doing so, we were forced to find ways to overcome those dangers. Prior to the 1950s, life was less certain, with higher infant mortality, fewer vaccinations, less work safety laws, and shorter life expectancies. It was not unusual for people to die from what we consider "everyday" activities today: childbirth, growing up, and work-related illnesses and dangers.

Those alive during that time lived through one of the most turbulent periods in modern Western history, and therefore, had a living memory of war, strife, and financial uncertainties, due to World War I, II, and the Great Depression. Today, we have become insulated, even mollycoddled, in every aspect of our lives, effectively denying ourselves stepping-stone opportunities to overcome our fears, increase our confidence, and gradually build individual and collective courage.

To illustrate this point, spend an evening watching television. About every 12-14 minutes we are shown a commercial selling us a product. The most fundamental precept of business marketing is that a product must solve a problem, even if a problem has to be created to solve. We are told about dangers (germs) lurking in every corner of our house, instilling in us a sense of fear, which, in turn, will lead us to buying products to kill those germs. To keep our family safe from germs, we are told to spray our kitchen counter tops with an anti-bacterial product, use hand-sanitizer before shaking hands, and use disinfectant wipes to clean a dog's muddy footprints off the floor. Oh, dear, never touch the toilet with your hands! Use this plastic stick to do the job...but please ignore the fact that the stick may spend hundreds of years in a landfill.

Fears are so embedded in our culture that it is hard to imagine life without those fears. Not long ago, my Irish-Catholic great-grandmother raised us to believe that a child wasn't healthy if they didn't eat a pound of dirt each year! While she worked as a cleaning woman for a local Catholic church, she was keenly aware of the role germs played in keeping us healthy. I doubt she really expected us to eat a pound of dirt, though it is a good metaphor for allowing children to be exposed to germs in order to build natural immunity.

Today, instead, we are told to do the exact opposite. We are encouraged to live in a sterile, sanitized environment. When we get sick, we are given pills to fix our health problems. Our physical bodies are under attack in the United States with direct-to-consumer (DTC) advertising, where healthcare companies advertise drugs directly to consumers, which is prohibited in most countries. Health is now a commodity, and it needs a fear to trigger a consumer purchase. *Do you have this symptom? Then ask your doctor to give you this pill.*

I became aware of the real danger of these types of advertisements when my six-year-old daughter informed me that she had a lack of motivation and was a bit tired. Catching me off-guard, she asked, "Mama, do you think I'm depressed?" At first, I thought, *Awwww! Isn't she so cute!* I shared the story with friends and family for a laugh.

Unknowingly, the more I re-told the story, the more I became angry. Unaware of what was fueling my anger, it took me several days to fully understand the source of my anger. When it became clear, I was fuming. I had let a clever marketing campaign instill a "feeling of less-than-perfect" in my daughter. Through the continual television advertisements, she had come to believe that something was wrong with her!

I could have easily told my daughter that there was nothing wrong with her and let it stop there. However, I decided that I could not stop the messaging she would encounter, but I could tell her the truth, or what I believed to be the truth. So I explained to her that companies need us to feel that something is wrong with us so that we buy their pills to fix the "problem."

I asked my daughter, "Do you know what a lack of motivation means?" She said, "Yes, I don't really like going to school." I explained to her, "Very few people really *like* going to school or work. Many people, including myself, would much rather stay at home and do fun things."

But we don't need a bloody pill for that! That's called *life*. I told her that there will be times when she will need medication for a health problem. But in this case, her issue was with life, and sometimes life requires us to do very hard things, or things that we really don't want to do, because we are not fully able to see the benefits of doing them at the time—like going to school.

As a parent with opened eyes, it has been an uphill battle reframing consumer messaging for my daughter. Now that she's a college student, and knowing my favorite movie is *The Matrix*, when I begin to reframe messaging, she often reminds me that she's taking the "blue pill" (to stay in the matrix). I tell her that I'm very sorry, but because I'd already taken the red pill (before she was conceived), she's already living outside the matrix with me. And I'm really, really sorry, but it's my job to help her see what she doesn't want to see. That's called being a parent. While she begrudgingly agrees with me, she always makes sure to remind me that she doesn't like agreeing with me.

Beyond germs or medication, our Western society has eliminated most real dangers from our everyday lives. In our sanitized world, it is difficult to distinguish a real danger from one that has been manufactured in order to get us to buy more products or prevent us from questioning the real dangers. This was brought home for me when my husband and I traveled to Ghana to source products for our fair trade store.

We stopped at a small food shack that was on the mouth of a river. As we sat there, we saw a group of children, probably no more than five to seven years old, coming to the shore to collect water for cooking in beaten up old buckets. One by one, they marched down the path, filled their buckets with water, placed them on their heads, and marched back through the thick grasses. The river water was used by the villagers for everything: bathing, cleaning, eating, eliminating bodily fluids, fishing, and disposing garbage. I sat there in shock as we watched them gather the water.

Suddenly, a great sadness filled me as I realized that the children collecting the water were about the same age as my daughter when she had asked me if I thought she was depressed. These children weren't worried about depression or taking a pill to fix it. They probably knew of the life-threatening dangers they faced every day by drinking the unclean water, but they had to do it in order to survive. Like my great-grandmother's generation, their survival was dependent on overcoming their fears on a daily basis.

I am not naïve enough to believe that if we stop watching television we will build courage. The problem is not the marketing gimmicks instilling fears of germs or depression. The real danger is in how we let fear stop us from jumping. I do believe, and I'm hopeful, that if we learn to identify our fears and create opportunities—not just to face our fears, but to overcome them—we will increase our confidence. We may then re-write the scripts in our belief system and build lifelong courage. With courage, we are able to make tough decisions, act on those decisions, take responsibility for our own lives, and live life to the fullest!

What Happens When We Don't Jump?

Our motivations, like us, change as we change. Therefore, each time we jump, we may have a different reason for doing so. Likewise, the reasons we jump today may or may not influence our decision to jump in the future. This is because, each opportunity to jump comes with its own encapsulated reasons, fears, and motivations. As much as we may want to use our past experiences as a guide, to help us make a future decision to jump, we would still find it difficult to do so. Similar to the reflecting patterns of a kaleidoscope, each jump is uniquely individual *and* dependent on our circumstances at that moment in time.

Herein lies the most fundamental truth about jumping: As we peer with one eye through our kaleidoscope of life, with all its uniquely complicated mix of reasons, fears, and motivations, we alone must make the decision to jump; no one can do it for us. Yes, others may influence us—either directly or indirectly. A loving or nagging spouse, a supportive or overbearing parent, an encouraging or discouraging teacher may lead us to a critical decision point—the cliff's edge. But the final decision to jump is always, always ours alone, as no one else can live our lives for us.

While our motivations are personal and situational, and uniquely ours, because of this fundamental, shared truth that we alone are responsible for making the decision to jump, the consequences for not jumping are *not* uniquely ours. The same consequences are shared by all of us, no matter the reason, circumstance, or situation. And there is no spoonful of medicine to make it more palatable.

In my opinion, the reason that we need to jump, even just once in our lives, is so we do not become a victim to our own life. We will never have full control over the people, events, and situations in our lives, but that does not mean we have no control in our lives. What we do have is choice. Jumping provides us the opportunity to exercise that choice in the face of fear. When we do not take the opportunity to overcome our fears and build lifelong courage, over time, our passivity takes away our choice—our choice to live the life that we want. Without exercising that choice, we slowly become helpless victims to the people, events, and situations in our lives.

Paraphrasing my cousin, she believes that: Each time we don't do something that we really wanted to do, or don't take a risk to change our lives, or simply don't give ourselves a chance, it's like we're burying ourselves alive. Following along these lines then, each time that we walk away from the cliff's edge when we needed to jump, we slowly add another morsel of earth to our living grave.

Jumping versus Not Jumping

Let's be clear. It is foolish to expect that every time we're presented with an opportunity to jump, we will actually jump. There are times when we need to step away from the edge—or hell, even run away as fast as we can. Sometimes having been to the cliff's edge was all that we needed to initiate a change in our perspective, and this may be as effective as jumping itself—with a lot less pain! Knowing when to jump and when not to jump are *both* equally important.

But that's not what we're talking about here though. What I mean is, when it is in our best interest to jump and we do not jump, we increase the likelihood that we will not jump the next time, or the time after that, and so forth. Over time, we may become paralyzed by fear, rendering us incapable of making simple life changes, let alone a big change.

When we are unable to make decisions for ourselves, the end result of this perpetual inaction is somewhat like death. It is the death of conscious living.

So what are your reasons for not jumping? When was the last time you passed up an opportunity to make a change and later regretted it? What do your regrets tell you about your decision not to jump?

Jumping versus Being Pushed

Let's imagine for a minute that you have found yourself, for whatever reason, at the cliff's edge. Perhaps it is the result of the dreaded sick feeling you wake up to every day, because of your toxic work environment. Most of your waking day and nighttime dreams are filled with fantasies of telling off your dictator-like boss, quitting your job, and walking out the door. Your friends and family are worried about you, as you are not eating regularly, you look tired, you are on-edge all the time, you can't relax, and you struggle to keep up your appearance.

Having recently found out that your 10-year-old daughter has a serious medical condition and needs surgery adds to your pressures. Your current job has an excellent health insurance plan, and you make enough money to live comfortably. It will be almost impossible to find another job with the same benefits and pay. Normally, your wife is very supportive of your needs, but she is now consumed with worry over your daughter's health. You feel guilty when she tells you to stick with your job, no matter what happens at work, because you'd be jeopardizing your daughter's health if you quit your job.

Or perhaps it is an abusive marriage that has led you to the cliff's edge. Your husband is an all-around nice person when he's not drinking. But when he drinks, he takes it out on you, demeaning you in front of the family. When he's drunk, he belittles you, telling you you're not strong enough to make it on your own. However, he doesn't realize he has a drinking problem.

The confidence you once had in yourself is a distant memory. You fear that your husband may try to harm you or your three young children if you try to leave. You stay, because you do not have the strength to challenge him. You try to convince yourself it is for the best; after all, it is better for your three children to have a father at home. But you are sick with worry all the time and your children know something is wrong.

Like the examples above, there will be times in our lives when there is no obvious way forward. Paralyzed with fear, we get stuck. We find ourselves at the cliff's edge, with two choices: jump or don't jump. If we don't jump, we step back from the edge and stay in our current situation, for better or worse.

We simply cannot find the courage to jump, as the risks seem too great. And stepping back from the edge is not an option either, as our situation is unbearable, and we feel that we do not have the power to change it. With all things being equal, you're standing at the edge of the cliff and desperately need to make a decision. Out of nowhere, an imaginary hand comes along and pushes you off the edge, forcing you to go over the edge. You are beyond grateful that the decision has been made for you, regardless of the outcome, because you did not have to make the decision yourself. Your sense of relief has jaded your ability to fully consider the consequences of being pushed. In this scenario, some may say: "I went over the cliff's edge. I went through all the motions. Surely this is the same as jumping?"

I really wish Julie Andrews was around with that spoonful of sugar to answer the question. Believe me, I'd love nothing more than to say that jumping and being pushed off a cliff's edge are the same thing. But having experienced firsthand the dreadfully terrible things that life can dish out—one on top of the other, until it seemed as though I could no longer bear it—I cannot and will not say it is that simple. To answer the question, jumping and being pushed are *not* the same thing. And here's why:

There are no shortcuts, no outs, no lessons learned in building courage if we do not make the decision ourselves to jump *and accept responsibility for the consequences.* It is my belief that if we are pushed, rather than jumping ourselves, the outcome will be altered to our disadvantage. While we may think we have experienced the same consequences whether we are pushed or we jump, we may have learned *other* lessons from the experience, so do not be fooled.

One of the first lessons we have learned is *not* accepting responsibility for making tough decisions for ourselves. This reinforces the belief that someone else will make decisions for us if we do not act. But most importantly, however, we have missed an opportunity: to build courage by overcoming our fears. And this lesson cannot be shortcutted or learned any other way, except by doing it firsthand. To illustrate this, let's look at the previous scenarios.

In the first example—the toxic work environment—let's imagine the husband went into work the next day and learned that his company was downsizing and laying off 25% of the staff. He sees his out and hopes he will be chosen for the layoff, seeing this opportunity as a triple win: he no longer has to "stick it out" with his abusive boss; he will be able to keep his insurance for a year, ensuring his daughter will still be able to get medical treatment; and best of all, he will not have to confront his wife as he would have had to do if he had made the decision to leave.

In the second example, let's imagine the wife comes home after work and her husband says he wants a divorce—he's met someone else. She is, at first, stunned, and had not seen it coming. Ultimately, she is relieved, but she's unsure about the challenges she and her children will now have living solely on her income. In her heart, she feels sorry for his new girlfriend, but more than anything, she is happy not to have had to stand up to her abusive, alcoholic husband.

In both scenarios, each went over the proverbial cliff's edge by being pushed, rather than making the decision to jump. As a result, neither took the opportunity to overcome their fears. Like jumping, both must live with the consequences of going over the cliff's edge. However, the difference comes back to *responsibility*. It is the single most valuable lesson I've learned from jumping.

When I make the decision to jump, no matter how hard and painful the consequences, it makes me a stronger person. Cynical people may say that jumpers have no one else to blame but ourselves. But I prefer to avoid "blaming" anyone, especially myself, as blame implies a negative outcome. Whatever the outcome, going through the process of facing my fears and overcoming them reinforces my confidence, strengthens my belief in myself, and gives me hope of a brighter future. When I get up after landing, I can look back and say, "I did it. I DID IT! I had the courage to face my fears, I was able to overcome them, and I have what it takes to do it again!"

Our lives are the direct result of our actions and inactions. Not making the decision to jump and being pushed, by letting someone do it for us, we deprive ourselves of taking responsibility for our actions, but most importantly, we deprive ourselves of the power of choice. Someone else has taken the power of choice away from us.

Attempting to skip over the "painful" parts—agonizing over the decision, facing the fear, finding the courage—we skip over the best part: the ultimate peace that we experience by making the decision ourselves and acting on it. Peace is replaced with doubt.

Yes, jumping and being pushed will both get us to the same place physically: the bottom of the cliff. However, jumping brings with it power, and being pushed takes away our power. Deceivingly, we may look the same on the outside, but our personal power is diminished. If we jump, we are courageous; if we are pushed, we are a victim.

Not every person who is forced into a situation, or pushed off a cliff, will ultimately become a victim, as we do not become victims overnight. However, each time that we are pushed (in other words, do not act on our own accord), we are writing a script in our belief system that reinforces our inaction.

Over time, this belief will strengthen. Waiting becomes our life story: waiting for someone else to make decisions for us, waiting for our situation to change, waiting for life to begin.

Instead, we must vigilantly seek opportunities to jump—starting off small, and working our way up to larger ones. We must learn to face our fears (not wish them away), evaluate our options, and make the best decisions that we can.

Knowing that many of us would rather be pushed, instead we must accept responsibility for our actions and learn to trust our decisions, so that we do not become victims to our own lives.

Let's imagine what it's like to jump:

You're standing at the edge of a cliff. Behind you is pain, turmoil, a life with no joy or peace. You've done everything in your power to change your situation. But you have come to realize that you cannot control others, only your own thoughts and actions.

In front of you is an opportunity. A chance to learn, to grow, to live life to the fullest—your fullest! You remind yourself of what you've been through to get here: the agonizing sleepless nights, the worry while facing your fears, and the constant doubt while evaluating your options. Then you remember the relief you felt, once you made the tough decision to jump, and the lightness it brought with it when the weight of the decision was finally lifted from your shoulders.

You know it will be hard after you jump, and it will require much determination to do so. It may even be the hardest thing you've ever done in your life. But in your heart, you know it will be rewarding. Taking this opportunity may 'hurt' the ones you love most, only because they see the situation differently than you do and want what they believe is 'best' for you.

However, you must do what you know you need to do to better your life.

You take one last look over the cliff's edge, and gather your nerves. You take a deep breath, clench your fists, close your eyes, and jump!

Once you land, you slowly open your eyes and stand up. You look around at this new place that is now your life, taking it all in: the unfamiliar sounds, smells, and people. You feel a little achy after landing, perhaps your legs feel a bit weak. But it will not stop you from taking that first step.

You dust yourself off and walk away, one step at a time.

You walk tall and proud, glowing from the inside out, because you did it.

YOU did it!

That felt good, right?

Why do We Need to Jump?

What Others Say about Jumping

Fahrenheit 451 author, Ray Bradbury, is attributed as the source for one of the more famous quotes about jumping off a cliff: "Jump off a cliff and build your wings on the way down." The quote has been cited by many—albeit, with slight variations. However, the underlying message is of letting go in order to release untapped creativity, by following our heart over our intellect, which gives us the courage to take risks.

Others have argued for the opposite view, offering different reasons why we should not jump. Some believe jumping can be a form of escapism. If we do not like our current situation, we should first realize that there are no quick fixes, and then work through our issues, one by one.

Another long-standing argument against jumping implies that we should not jump just because someone else has jumped: "If you saw (fill in the person's name) jump off a bridge, would you jump too?" In a similar vein: "If I told you to jump off a bridge, would you do it?" This implies that we are doing it as a result of peer-pressure—as if seeing someone else jump, or having someone tell us to jump, influences us into taking a risk that we are not prepared to take. This infers that we are not thinking for ourselves.

The arguments for not jumping are based on the perception that jumping is a negative thing to do. Limited in their assessments on jumping, these simple sayings or arguments against jumping do not discuss any benefits or positive outcomes that may be derived from jumping.

While I do agree with some of their reasons for not jumping, as I strongly believe we must make the decision to jump for ourselves, jumping is not about escaping or avoiding thinking for ourselves. Jumping can be an enriching, life-affirming experience.

How we view jumping and the final outcome of our jump is *always* our choice. And that choice is expressed through our actions and our inactions, equally.

Personal Benefits of Jumping

So far, I've laid out many reasons why we need to jump, which include:

- ❖ Building confidence in different situations
- ❖ Reinforcing our belief in ourselves
- ❖ Increasing the likelihood that we will do it again
- ❖ Using hope to find the courage to make tough decisions, and knowing that overcoming fears is an opportunity for personal growth
- ❖ Writing or re-writing the scripts in our belief system, and creating a powerful life story
- ❖ Avoiding becoming a victim to our own life, by taking responsibility for our actions and inactions
- ❖ Gaining a deep sense of accomplishment
- ❖ Instilling a belief in our own personal power

While this is quite an impressive list, it is by no means exhaustive.

What other benefits would you add to the list?

Collective Benefits of Jumping

Similar to tossing a stone into a calm body of water, our actions have an impact on others around us. Therefore, when one of us takes a jump, it may influence others—in ways that we may not have imagined. Unknowingly, we may become a living example for others.

This is not to be mistaken for peer-pressure, which encourages others to avoid taking responsibility for their actions. Yet, if we set positive examples of jumping, it encourages others to consciously reevaluate their options. Sometimes, it may simply encourage others to see a situation differently. Or, our jumping may help others to have hope, and with that hope they may find the courage to jump.

Prior to leaving my job to grow my business, I thought I was the only one suffering from job-related stress. I felt alone and that something was wrong with me. I thought I was different in a negative way, believing myself to be the only one who couldn't cope with the stress and everyone else was fine. I imagined that my fellow co-workers were, for the most part, fulfilled and content with their jobs.

After putting in my two-weeks notice, and it became public knowledge that I would be leaving my very well-paid job to run my own business, I feared I'd become the laughing stock of the department. What happened was altogether different. Some co-workers came to see me out of curiosity about my decision. People who rarely, or never, spoke to me came to congratulate me. More people than I could have imagined said positive things. No one thought I was crazy.

Not wanting to glamorize what I was doing, because it wasn't as though I was starting a major scientific business. I was, after all, leaving a secure, well-paid job to run a retail store, and fair trade at that, which meant even less money.

So I developed an expression that summed up my reasons: "Leaving for bluer skies, not greener pastures." It was amazing making new connections with people I'd worked with for years and never really knew. People began to tell me about their passions, what they loved to do, and their dreams for future businesses. They told me how I had got them thinking. Some told me I had given them hope.

For as long as I had the retail business, many would visit me at the store to continue sharing their stories with me. They shared stories about life and work, new relationships, transfers to new departments, layoffs and relocations, new businesses, exciting adventure holidays, and so on. I cannot express, without sounding totally corny, how much their supportive words and our newly forged relationships meant to me—both then and now.

As lovely as this sounds, including the positive strokes to our egos, we must never jump for others. We must jump for own benefit, and when it is best for us to do so. And by doing this, we might set a positive example that may inspire others to make positive changes to their lives too.

When was the last time your actions positively impacted those around you? To help you remember, think about all the relationships you have in your life: partner, spouse, children, parents, co workers, friends, as well as those who you see in church and while doing hobbies and activities. Have you influenced any of these people?

Know that when we jump, we create ripples.

CHAPTER 4

GRANDMA RITA'S JUMPING GEAR

When we least expect it, life sets us a challenge to test our courage and willingness to change; at such a moment, there is no point in pretending that nothing has happened or in saying that we are not ready.

The challenge will not wait. Life does not look back. A week is more than enough time for us to decide whether or not to accept our destiny.

Paulo Coelho

Who is Grandma Rita?

Life gives us many treasures. Some come nicely wrapped in brightly colored paper with bows. We can easily recognize them as gifts to be treasured and are excited when we receive them. Some treasures come wrapped in sharp, thorny spikes, making it nearly impossible to get too close to them without risking injury, so we may not see them as gifts to be treasured. Whether it is the fear of getting hurt, or we are too busy with the running of our own lives, we do not open them and enjoy the receipt of their gift. When they are gone, only then may we begin to fully recognize their value. Only then do we see how truly important they were to us.

As a 23-year-old newlywed, I stood hand-in-hand, crying with my mother and uncle, at my Grandmother Rita's bedside and watched my anchor, my protector, take her last breath. It was, and still is after twenty years, the most painful yet loving experience I have ever witnessed in my life.

Her death mirrored her life: a heady mix of misery and joy. More than anyone else, I received greater joy than misery from her, as I was her favorite. She invested dearly in me so that I would have a future brighter than the women spanning generations in my family. I loved her as best as my youthful self could, despite the spikes, which there were many.

My Grandma Rita was a 3-packs-a-day, all-day-coffee-drinking woman with a hardened exterior, thickened by a lifetime of suffering: a childhood in the hills of a small coalmining town during the Great Depression, a post-war marriage to an abusive Protestant, delayed childbearing at a time when it wasn't cool to wait, struggles to be a supportive mother (and, at times, failing), the impermanence of keeping possessions from being broken or stolen, financial insecurities and infidelities, continual moving, and if that wasn't enough, being the mother of an unwed pregnant daughter in 1969, who got kicked out of high school because she was having a black baby.

My birth was no gift wrapped in brightly colored paper either. In reality, it was another burden to add to my Grandma Rita's already heavy load. But that wasn't how she viewed me or her life. She persevered until her last breath.

Hidden in Plain Sight

Under her thickened layers, my Grandma Rita was, beyond a doubt, a loving and protective mother and grandmother, and she viewed nothing "beneath" her when it came to keeping us safe and fed. The "us" consisted of my mother (a teenage, unwed mother of a mixed-race child; ardent alcoholic who always fell for the drug dealers; and a waitress who worked her fingers to the bone while serving others their food), my uncle (with beautiful, Robert Plant/Huey Lewis-like blond hair and blue eyes, closer in age to me than my mother, yet, despite his golden locks, fought his mental demons), and me (an abortion-surviving miracle child turned overachiever, who believed herself undeserving of the gift of life and, therefore, could not "screw up," so she learned early on to hide her "dirty laundry" while swallowing other people's pain).

Taking care of us, to say the least, was a challenge. While my Grandma Rita did her best to hide it from us, hurt and disappointment were her constant companions. But I can tell you, unlike us, she neither minced words, nor told us things we wanted to hear just to make us feel better. She told it like it was, or at the very least, the way she saw it. I can still see her in my mind's eye, sitting at her "retro" kitchen table behind a cup of Folgers, with a large, round, nearly full plastic ashtray in front of her, and a cigarette wagging between her first and second fingers, telling us exactly how it was. And "how it was" often had to do with shit!

We were always reminded of what happens when "you shit in one hand," or if you can't shit, or what you have to do if somebody—or life—is shitting on you. Like my grandmother, her expressions and lessons weren't sugar-coated to make them more palatable; they were wrapped in a lifetime of pain, and came out so quickly and so often that eventually we all stopped listening. We were unable to hear her or her words of wisdom. It was as if her pain-coated words, dripping with *shite*, were dropped on deaf ears and laid waiting to be discovered sometime later—truths hidden in plain sight! They, like her, persevered.

Delayed Decoding

Her words have always stayed with me, echoing in the halls of my earliest memories. Sometimes, in the early morning hours, half-awake, half-dreaming, I hear the sound of her voice. And I can remember the occasions that gave rise to the words.

Amazingly, after thirty-five years, I can still feel, with razor-sharp clarity, the piercing edge of disappointment in her tone.

Unfortunately, my grandmother did not get to meet or know my sober mother—a somber consequence of sobriety, garnered from a death that came too soon and too sudden.

While my grandmother's words have been with me all these years, the wisdom that they carried did not reveal themselves to me until my last jump. Perhaps it took that much time to walk a mile in her shoes in order to fully understand their good sense.

Prior to this last jump—my move to England—three of her sayings helped me more than any others. Like a broken record, I said them over and over when I needed to get through a difficult time. Or, they have been recited back to me by my loving husband, who also uses them to support me. They have been beacons of light, guiding me through darkness, giving me hope and strength to find the courage to make it when I believed I could not.

Heartbreakingly, I'd jumped from abuse, addictions, poverty, people I loved dearly, "safety net" jobs, unhealthy situations, and from following my dreams.

Looking back at those jumps—each individual and unique in their own way—her words universally helped me, no matter the circumstance. Yet, I still viewed her words as one-dimensional life lessons repeating on a broken record player. Taking them only at face value, I was unable to peel back their layers to uncover their deeper meaning.

This jump, however, changed that. Four weeks after our move to England, feelings of unimaginable grief and despair hit me like a ton of bricks, along with a host of mysterious illnesses. Despite the doctors' assurances that it was only temporary—a result of the move and the damp weather—and I'd feel better in the spring, I could not stop crying as I attempted to empty an endless supply of sorrow. It was a powerful combination of self-pity—for all I'd willingly and unwillingly given up—and feeling punished—because the move was a lot harder than I'd expected, and I had not planned to start my whole life over.

This was all topped off with a healthy dose of deep resentment, because of my age. I held the belief that life was supposed to get easier by my mid-40s—not harder. And if that wasn't enough, I had unrelenting hurt in my body: painfully swollen fingers, achy elbows and shoulders, throbbing joints, anxiety, an endless rising and falling pit in my stomach, panic attacks, headaches, asthmatic coughs, colds, and sweaty nights. I really thought I was losing it—in the old-fashioned way when they send people away. I prayed for the Divine Creator to take me—somewhere, anywhere; just take the pain away.

After two solid months of virtual non-stop crying, only pulling it together long enough to talk with my mother or daughter, or to go on interviews for yet another job that I'd be denied, I woke up one morning and saw my grandmother's sea-blue eyes smiling down on me from my mind's eye. In my darkest hour, her words breathed new life, took on new meaning, became multidimensional, and gave shape to a fuller understanding. Formed out of pain, they were now filled with a substance I had not known before.

However, I am fairly certain that my grandmother did not intentionally mean these words in the way that I have decoded them, for the opposite was probably the case. In many ways, she used them like words of weapons: to hurt us, by reminding us of her pain. What I have come to realize, however, regardless of her intention, in her heart, I know that she would never have wanted to intentionally hurt us. Whereas she had governance over her intention for saying the words, those of us who heard them governed how we received them—meaning, the impact of any spoken word belongs to the listener, and is filtered through their lens of life; therefore, the intention and interpretation may be completely different.

By jumping, crashing, and completely destroying who I thought I was, I also destroyed many long-held beliefs that I had: who I was, what I wanted, and what was most important to me; they were now gone. So when I heard my grandmother's words in my mind's eye, this time I was finally able to listen with my soul's ears.

This is what I heard…

Stop Crying and Open your Eyes, Child

In my experience, the most difficult part in jumping is making the final decision to jump. The mental exhaustion can be brutal. We are simultaneously dealing with fears—both imagined and real—that come to the surface to be healed, and weighing the pros and cons of each of our options, while searching under every rock for an ounce of courage to make the decision.

If that isn't enough to deal with, we are doing all of these things in an impossibly stressful situation. It is this very situation that has slowly led us to the cliff's edge in the first place. Few of us go to the cliff's edge willingly, without a fight.

Don't get me wrong—it is not all doom and gloom. We should actively seek moments of joy when we can, giving ourselves time to catch our breath and enjoy a moment of peace—a "breather." But again, that is an active choice that we have to make, as these moments usually do not occur if we do not create them for ourselves. By creating these moments, we give our mind and body a break from the stress. It is often during these "breathers" that we are able to objectively view our situation and find creative solutions.

There will be many other equally challenging times once the decision to jump has been made. It is by no means a walk in the park. If it were easy, everyone would be jumping. Once the decision to jump has been made, there are two ways to go over the cliff: with or without opening a parachute. Some have also likened the parachute to a pair of wings that we grow on the way down, as in Bradbury's quote. Fundamentally, the parachute and wings convey the same concept: to help us land safely.

For my last jump, I had landed safely with the use of an open parachute, albeit aided by my grandmother's one-dimensional "uncoded" words. For over twenty years they have helped me, through three major jumps and countless minor jumps. Four weeks after "landing" in England, I metaphorically put my parachute aside, moments before the bottom fell out from beneath me. Within the blink of an eye, the ground was gone. Since I had not anticipated this false bottom, I was not prepared for what was to come. There was no parachute to open, nor any Balm of Gilead to ease the pain from the first landing. Once I hit the real bottom, I was completely broken. It was from this bottom, two months later, when I heard my grandmother tell me to open my eyes.

It was a gradual process of discovery, accompanied by major crying spells that lessened over a six month period. Rebuilding a new life is not an overnight process. It takes time and requires much patience. While each day presented new challenges, I was, however, getting stronger, and could see more clearly without the blurred distortion of my tears.

My first discovery was that my grandmother's sayings had a logical sequence. Much like a Japanese puzzle box, they had an order that could be fashioned into steps: steps 1, 2, and 3.

Once they were nicely lined up, their deeper meanings revealed themselves, opening like the petals of a lotus flower, each giving up their treasures, their double meanings.

Over the next three months, it was almost as if my grandmother herself was whispering secret-coded messages into my ear each morning, helping me once again.

The following steps are my Grandmother Rita's sayings that were hidden in plain sight for over twenty-five years, like secret-coded messages waiting for me to decode them. They have saved me after this last jump, by opening my eyes, releasing me from fear, and helping me to find the courage to live life again. Her pain-coated words have been transformed into a lifesaving parachute that we can all use to safely land after jumping.

Thank you, Grandma! I miss you so very much!

Love,
Mar

Step 1 – Wish in One Hand, Shit in the Other

Most of my conversations and interactions with my grandmother focused on day-to-day necessities: getting money, getting food, paying bills, getting rides to and from work, determining my mother's whereabouts, and getting my mother's money before she spent it at the bar. Money was, by far, the most discussed, as we were always struggling to find more, and my grandmother was always struggling with plans for our family's future needs, usually without our awareness. She spent her time and energy on practical matters—getting things done—and, therefore, had little patience for "bullshitters," or our flippant comments about things we didn't have. So whenever we came to my grandmother complaining, or wishing for something other than what we had, in her unflinching way, she'd say: "Wish in one hand and shit in the other, and see which one fills up fastest."

My earliest thoughts, when I'd heard her say this, were simply, *gross!* As a young child, I remember thinking to myself, *Who in their right mind would shit in their hand?* I later tried to work it out in my mind, thinking, *How does one actually shit in their own hand? Is it even physically possible? That's just plain disgusting!* As a teenager, my curiosity turned to cynicism, and I became angry with my grandmother, because she never let us focus on what we didn't have—which was a lot, most of the time. I thought she was a negative, mean person for squelching our dreams, or what I believed to be dreams.

Like our two hands, I have come to realize that there is *always* more than one way of looking at something. Sometimes there are two ways, and sometimes there are hundreds of ways, as my husband often reminds me when I narrowly focus on only two options.

Creating a Crystal Clear Vision

Without a doubt, the most important step in making a life change, or jumping, is setting a crystal clear vision of what we want to achieve from jumping. Putting it into context: "Wish in one hand." If we do not have a crystal clear vision of what we want, we will not achieve it, nor will we recognize our own success if we have not yet defined what it will look like. To determine our vision, we should ask ourselves: *What do we hope to accomplish from jumping? How do we envision our life after the jump? What are we doing?*

To be clear, I am not speaking of superficial wishes, such as: a new car, a new house, a new job, or more money.

Unfortunately, wishing, dreaming, and fantasizing are synonymously viewed negatively, so much so that we are often discouraged from engaging in these seemingly wasteful pastimes. Sharing our deepest desires with others, especially with our loved ones, can be met with resistance, as our desires may be incorrectly interpreted, or imply that we are not satisfied or happy with our lives or the material objects that we have, and because of that unhappiness or dissatisfaction, we want something different. This is partly true, but also partly not true.

In my experience, often these internal stirrings are symptomatic of a deeper unfulfilled need, and allowing ourselves the space to dream, wish, or fantasize about our desires, can help us to understand them, and by extension, enable us to meet needs that we are not consciously aware of at the time. While I cannot offer a professional opinion, it is my personal belief that when we do not address underlying needs, we are more likely to engage in self-destructive behaviors—almost acting out against ourselves.

By giving ourselves permission to responsibly indulge in these creative thoughts, we are one step closer to better understanding our deeper, unmet needs. Responsibly indulging means: we wholeheartedly believe and accept that it is our responsibility alone, and not our loved ones', to meet our underlying, unmet needs. It is our duty to ourselves to better understand our reasons for wanting.

To determine the underlining need, we should ask ourselves: *Is our wanting actually a need for security, acceptance, stability, love? What is the underlying fear that is creating the desire in the first place? Is it rejection, instability, loneliness? Is there a higher-level need wanting to be expressed, such as an untapped potential, creativity, or life purpose? Is there a fear of not living up to our full potential? Do we fear not living up to others' expectations, or letting them down?*

Whatever the cause or reason for wanting something that we don't have, the truth is, the nature of life is to change; therefore, we, ourselves, are constantly changing. Life demands change—sometimes little by little, sometimes in great leaps and bounds. As such, our needs, wants, and desires will change. What motivates us to act today will be different tomorrow, as a result of internal changes within our control and external changes outside of our control.

The challenge in meeting our own needs is balancing our needs with our loved ones' needs, while keeping our feet firmly rooted in reality. For instance, if we find ourselves up against an impossible situation—at work, in our marriage, or with our personal growth—we cannot simply quit our job, walk out of our marriage, or snap our fingers to reinvent ourselves overnight into the person we hope to be. Despite our desire for instant gratification, nothing happens overnight. Making change happen takes time.

Admittedly, this is my hardest challenge as an overachiever. I have difficulty staying grounded, because I often feel a heavy responsibility for helping others, which then leads me to overestimating what I can reasonably accomplish in a given time, so I push myself to exhaustion, in the end harming myself.

With maturity I have learned to continually question my motivations for making a change: *How does my motivation and desire for the change impact myself and others? Is the benefit of the change worth the disruption caused by making the change? What is it that drives me to want the change? What do I hope to achieve from it?* Asking myself, *why?* over and over again, I aim to get to the underlying reason for my desire for the change, the purpose of the change, the outcome I hope to achieve, and the cost of the change—both to me and my loved ones.

Once I understand the purpose of my change, I then relate it back to existing aspects of my life. At the end of the day, our lives are a series of planned and unplanned events, routines, habits, and other activities. All of these activities are like building blocks that construct our day-to-day lives. So when we begin to construct a vision of our changed lives, the simplest way to create that vision is envisioning and incorporating one building block at a time: ourselves, our families, our friends, our home life, our pets, our work, our fun, our personal growth, and so on.

So when I say to set a crystal clear vision of the change, consider the following questions: *What do you hope to achieve from the change? How does the change fit into your existing, everyday life? How many "blocks" will be affected by the changes you want to make? How many blocks can you change at the same time and still maintain stability in your life? How do you see your day-to-day life going?*

When you create your vision, think practically. Think small blocks, such as: waking, the start and end of the day, work, home life, social life, weekends, fitness, health, meals, commuting, interests, hobbies, vacations, fun time, and growth and development opportunities. These are the basic building blocks of life—not a fantasy Hollywood life that is overflowing with fake situations, unrealistic lives, overemphasized materialistic gains, and unattainable goals.

When you replay your vision, pay attention to the details: What do you look like? What are you feeling (avoid using the word "happy")? Are you laughing, crying, or smiling? Where do you live? What does your home look like? Where do you work? What are you achieving? Did you create something? Did you build or fix something? Are you fulfilled by your efforts? Are you working hard until you sweat? How do you see yourself with your children? Are you participating in activities with them, or sitting on the sidelines? Are you providing a structured, loving, and supportive home? Imagine the taste of the food you're cooking. Imagine the vacations you take…where do you go? Imagine the exciting, mind-blowing sex you have….

Picture living the life that you want to live, block by block. *Wish in one hand.*

Eliminating What Doesn't Fit in the Vision

If my grandmother, in her heart, really wanted us to stop wishing, if she really wanted us to accept her pain-coated words at face value, then there is no way I would be where I am today: writing this book. It is because she contradicted herself, and wished and dreamed of something that did not seem possible, that I was able to break many family cycles of abuse, alcoholism, lack of education, drug addiction, and smoking—just to name a few. She knew, above all else, that we must eliminate those things that do not serve us, even if it is our own family.

When I withdrew from the Penn State Electrical Engineering program to move to New York City to live with my ex-husband, then-boyfriend, we had big ambitions and little money; in fact, we struggled for many years. He worked two—sometimes three—jobs after he completed his degree, and I worked full-time as a secretary, while taking evening and weekend classes. Like us, my grandmother had a plan of her own, and that was to keep me from coming back home.

She did all she could to support me in my new life. She convinced my mother, who had never flown on an airplane before, to fly to New York to visit me. A few years later, my grandmother arranged for my family to travel to New York for my wedding. When I mistakenly thought I was pregnant, six months after getting married, my grandmother planned to come and take care of the baby so that I could finish my degree. She sent care packages of essentials, VHS tapes of *All My Children*, and as much money as she could afford.

Unaware of her personal agenda, my mother only told me about my grandmother's plan during the writing of this book. My grandmother had told my mother that she never wanted me to come back home, saying, "There is nothing good for her [me] here," only bad things. At the time, I did not know of my grandmother's plans to keep me from coming home. As a 19-year-old, essentially estranged from my family, struggling to find my way in the world, all I knew was: I was tired, I was burnt out, and I could not live like that anymore.

So the other half of the equation when creating a vision: eliminating what does not fit, is equally as important as deciding how we want our life, before we make a jump. It represents the second half of the expression: *Shit in the other hand.* It may sound callous, unfeeling, unsympathetic, or harsh, putting it that way, however, eliminating toxins from our body is vitally important to our physical wellbeing. Equally vital to our emotional, mental, and spiritual wellbeing is eliminating toxic activities, habits, people, and situations, or at the very least, limiting our exposure to them.

Like all things, some things are easier to get rid of than others. The trick is to identify the things that are preventing us from fulfilling our wishes and eliminate them.

The most wonderful part is, size does not matter. The beauty in eliminating even a small item, makes it easier to eliminate bigger ones. Doing so will have an exponentially cumulative effect on our confidence. It is a lot like losing weight: the first five pounds may be the hardest to lose, but once lost, those pounds encourage us to stay the course, helping us to lose the next pound, and the next.

By focusing on small, bite-sized chunks, the task seems more manageable, and leads to the proverbial "domino effect." When a cumulative effect is reached—say we've lost thirty pounds and reached our goal—we may then find the courage to eliminate more difficult hindrances in our lives.

There will be times when we are faced with only impossible choices, such as, we cannot find a solution to get out of a harmful situation. In my situation, it was much easier for me to move away from my mother. It fit into the natural order of life. Firstly, as a young adult, it was expected at my age. Secondly, I was an adult child.

If I were in my grandmother's shoes, having two adult children who were emotionally, physically, and financially dependent on me, the answers would not have been as clear.

It can be heartbreaking to walk away from loved ones. We cannot simply move away from loved ones who depend on us for their survival. Neither can we quit our jobs if we do not have something else lined up, no matter how toxic the environment—especially if we have children who are dependent on us for their care. So how do we eliminate the toxins in our life when we can't remove ourselves from the situation?

Unfortunately, I cannot tell you the answer to that question, nor would I attempt to. What I can say is this: We are not compartmentalized individuals—we are complex, integrated, holistic beings—so when we eliminate something in one area of our life, it may have a profound and life-changing effect on other areas of our lives.

To that end, when we are unable to jump from one area, by changing in another area of our life—one that we *do* have the ability to change—we may perceive differently the area that we cannot eliminate.

What I can tell you with certainty is: There is no one way, right way, or wrong way; there is only *your way*. No one can tell us what is right for us, or how to live our life. We must make our own decisions and accept the responsibility for those decisions, while building confidence, believing in ourselves, and finding hope and courage to make a change, when life forces us to change, and when it's necessary to jump.

Most importantly, there is *always* a way. And no matter the size of the jump, the principles are the same.

When we eliminate the things that do not serve us— participating in addictions, acting out, putting ourselves down, eating unhealthy, overeating, holding onto weight that keeps us tired, watching too much television, drinking too much, smoking, taking drugs, replaying negative thoughts, or manipulating, controlling, or harming others—there is one less thing between us and our dream. When we eliminate even one small item, we take one step closer to making our wishes come true.

Just imagine life free from things that keep us down: addictions, negative thoughts, harmful relationships. Can you see yourself doing the things that you wish for? What would your life look like if you lived it based on freedoms—instead of fears? How much time and money would you have, and what if you only spent it on people and things that matter to you the most?

Listen to Grandma Rita, by wishing in one hand and shitting in the other. Take comfort in the fact that one is filling up faster. Know that you can be one step closer to making your wishes come true!

Step 2 – Right or Wrong, Just Make a Decision

When I look at my grandmother's life now, through my mid-life lens, and speculate on how she may have felt, based on our shared traits, her actions, and her sayings, I believe she viewed people in two broad categories: those who could make decisions and those who could not. It was clear that she had little patience for those who couldn't.

My grandfather and my mother, being in the latter category, were notorious for their inability to make even the most basic decision. My grandmother's mother, Velma (my great-grandmother), would often use a house painting analogy to illustrate the differences between my grandfather and grandmother: "Jol would still be at the kitchen table with a cup of coffee, thinking about a color, and Rita would've already painted the house."

Time and time again, my great-grandmother would tell the same story to highlight my grandmother's much admired determination: she would have already made the decision (to paint the house), got the tools that she needed to get the job done (bought the paint), and completed the task (painted the entire house) in the time that it took my grandfather to decide on a color.

Since my grandparents divorced shortly after I was born, I can only remember my grandmother's frustrations with my mother's inability to make a decision. Still freshly echoing in my mind's ear, I can hear my angry grandmother's words: *Right or wrong, Sandra, just make a decision!*

Before my last jump, this saying was already a well-played "you have to do it" mantra. For years, I repeated it over and over in my head, primarily using it as a motivational tool whenever I was faced with making a tough decision, similar to a coach repeating encouraging words to their players.

My grandmother and I both share the same persistent determination and "get on with it" attitude when it comes to making decisions. Unlike my grandmother, however, I struggled with smaller, what-to-cook-for-dinner decisions.

While the saying was not new to me, it too laid waiting, coated in painful memories, for me to decode its secret meaning.

Delving into its layers, I searched for its deeper meaning, dissecting the inherent underlying reasons as to why we fail to make decisions, and the undeniable consequences when we do not make them.

More fundamentally, however, I wanted to better understand the "right or wrong" qualifier. In other words, how our judgments affect our decisions.

Returning from my search, it was evident that this saying had a bigger part to play than simply being my own personal tape-recorded life coach telling me "you have to do it." I decided that making a decision may seem to be an obvious, yet critical, step when making a change that it "goes without saying," but because of fear, we often overlook this step, or deny it, by pretending the problem will go away on its own accord. Sometimes we agonize over making the decision, so much so that we become paralyzed, unable to do it in the end.

When we find ourselves at the cliff's edge, essentially we are faced with three options—the first two options representing opposite ends of the spectrum. The first option is: we return from the cliff's edge and accept our situation "as is." I call this the "total acceptance" option. With this option, we make no internal or external changes, and do not consider the cost that going back may have on us—mentally, physically, emotionally, or spiritually. The second option is to jump. We first make a conscious decision to make a major change, and then we make the change.

The last option is probably the most common, as it can be viewed as the "easiest" of the three options. We attempt to alter or slightly modify our situation so that it is manageable, bearable. I call this the "middle ground" option. We attempt to change the things that we can and accept the things that we can't change, similar to the approach advocated by Alcoholics Anonymous in the *Serenity Prayer.* Accept the things I cannot change, change the things I can, and have the wisdom to know the difference.

If we choose the third option, more often than not, the changes we are able to make are internal (our thoughts, feelings, and actions), as they are within our control. External changes—those outside our control (people, places, and situations)—are more difficult to affect. If we were able to easily make external changes, we probably would not have found ourselves at the cliff's edge in the first place.

When we change our perception of our situation, it may just be the catalyst that we need to make necessary adjustments to ensure our wellbeing. We may go from telling ourselves: *"This is bad. I can't take it anymore,"* to: *"This isn't so bad. I think I can handle it a little longer,"* or: *"It's hard, but I think I can make it work if I do* this *instead of* that."

Since this simple "self-talk" may seem too easy, we may be tempted to think it doesn't work. Do not be fooled. Again, everything boils down to our scripts and the strength of our belief in them. Once we are able to change our thinking about our situation, we will be able to take action, or at least not feel as hopeless, powerless, or stressed about our current situation.

Whichever option we choose, there is no escaping the unavoidable reality: *We must make a decision to jump or not to jump.*

It was as if I could hear my grandmother's voice whispering into my half-asleep, half-dreaming ear, saying, "This is the next thing to do after shitting in one hand and wishing in the other. Just make a decision, right or wrong."

After creating a crystal clear vision of what we want, and eliminating those things that do not fit into our vision, we must face the music by asking ourselves, "*What are we going to do about it?*" Or, as my Grandmother Rita would say, "Just make a decision, right or wrong!"

Why are Decisions so Hard to Make?

We know deep down inside that making a decision is unavoidable, and not making a decision is still making a decision—the decision not to act. So either way, we are making a choice to either act or not to act.

But what is it about making a final decision, a final *yes* or *no*, that renders the task so hard? The bottom line is: Making a decision forces us to commit to a choice and to accept a certain level of finality in the outcome—an outcome that we may or may not fully know when making the decision. This ambiguity between the choice and the outcome can make us feel uncomfortable, vulnerable.

In my experience, the level of difficulty in making a decision is directly related to our fear that is associated with the outcome (*Will this outcome force me out of my comfort zone? If so, how far?*), our desire for a specific outcome (*How much do I want* this *to happen and not* that? *Will I be able to accept it if what I don't want to happen happens instead of what I want to happen?*), the level of risk we are willing to accept (*Will I be okay if such and such should happen?*), and the irreversible nature of the choice (*Can I change my mind afterwards, or will I be stuck with the outcome?*).

Generally speaking, the greater the risk to ourselves and to our loved ones, the harder the decision will be to make. Choosing where we go on vacation with multiple desired outcomes—say, the Caribbean or the Canaries—is significantly easier than making the decision to leave an abusive marriage with young children, where the risks are numerous and hurting loved ones is inevitable. With several significant factors to consider, it is not surprising that making a decision is extremely difficult, and at times, seemingly impossible.

At the heart of making a decision is confidence and beliefs, which take us back to what was discussed earlier. By having confidence and supportive beliefs—that is, scripts in our belief system that encourage us to overcome our fears—we may begin to trust our decisions.

Freeing ourselves from the gripping power that our fears may have on us, and working from a foundation of trust in ourselves, we can objectively assess our options and weigh the risks. This will, in turn, allow us to accept a greater level of risk, the irreversible nature of our choice (as jumping is generally irreversible), and lastly, the finality of our choice (the outcome). Accepting the final outcome is required in order for us to move forward after we land (we'll discuss this further in Chapter 6: "Landing Safely").

Each time that we go through the process of making a decision about our lives, our ability to make decisions in the future is strengthened. As with all things, it may come more naturally for some than for others. Rest assured, however, learning to make decisions, and trusting in the decisions that we make, is a learned skill that can be mastered by anyone with the desire to do so.

Without sounding like a broken record, there is a reoccurring theme here: the more we actively make decisions—starting off with smaller, less risky ones, and growing into more challenging decisions—we create powerful scripts in our belief system, and over time, the scripts will strengthen, providing us with a wellspring of confidence and helping us to trust our decisions. Lastly, and most importantly, it gives us what we need in order to do it again and again: courage.

Now that I've laid the foundation for making decisions—making a decision is a critical step in jumping, there are factors that make it more difficult to make a decision, and how our confidence, beliefs, hope, and courage have a say in our decisions—it is time to turn our attention to our judgments. All too often we allow our judgments to wreak havoc in our lives—by instilling fears in us and stopping us from consciously making decisions.

To be or Not to be Right? That is the Question!

As unique and individual as we are as people, so too are our judgments on ourselves, others, and situations. Each of us has a complicated set of values that defines what we believe to be right or wrong, good or bad. We get our values from our parents, extended families, tribes, clans, communities, society, and the media.

Some judgments are "inherited," so to speak, originating from our upbringing and passed down to us before our age of awareness, while others grow out of our own life experiences. All of our values shape and mold what we think is acceptable behavior, becoming judgments when we relate (or apply) our values to ourselves, others, and situations.

These values define what we, ourselves, are willing to accept, and what we view is acceptable for others. Once a value has been established, it is continually reinforced by those who instilled it in us, and by our own selective filtering of information; meaning, when we assess a situation, we may selectively pick and choose only the information that supports our judgments, and ignore information that challenges our judgments.

Because of this, our ability to change our values becomes harder to do. We may become less likely to change our thinking ("narrow-minded"), and not allow ourselves to be open to other ways of thinking ("open-minded").

No such values are more rigid than our views on marriage, religion, cultural identity, and ethnicity, as these are our most fundamental, shared life experiences—that which connects us to, or separates us from, one another.

If, for example, we are born into a deep-rooted religious family, we would be expected to marry another person of the same religion, and often of the same cultural or ethnic background. Marrying someone outside our religion and background would be clearly viewed as "wrong" or "bad."

In addition to these family values, we also develop an intricate web of social-based values that influence our views and decisions on how we live our lives. These include: parenting, professions, career choices, relationships, economic status, and self-image—just to name a few!

Today, we have an increased awareness of our "self." We live with a constant backdrop of pressure to promote our "self," as a result of social media, the cult of celebrity, the objectification of women, and what some call the "rise of narcissism."

These social values can heavily influence what we deem to be right or wrong, good or bad, as others' view of us may factor in our decisions. When making a decision, we may ask ourselves: *If I make this decision, will I still look good to others? Will I be liked by my friends, fans, and followers?*

What values—from your childhood, family, and friends—do you believe support you in making conscious decisions? What values do you find the hardest to live within? What values have stopped you from making an important decision? Do you regret not making that decision? What would you do differently if others had no say in your decision or were unaware of your decision?

Breaking Down Barriers

Values provide us with a framework for our most fundamental human need: to feel safe and secure. We may feel more comfortable when we live up to a standard that is accepted by others. Unfortunately, when inherited and learned judgments govern our decisions and affect our actions, they may also deprive us from living a conscious life.

What happens if we accept that living has inherent risks, and we move away from the need to feel safe and secure? What happens if we actively make decisions based on our internal motivations and reasons, even if it goes against our values? This is what happens: We break down barriers for ourselves and others, barriers that may have stopped us in the past; we begin to re-write our internal scripts that had once told us that what we wanted to do was right or wrong, good or bad; and we begin to enjoy the freedom of living a conscious life that is based on our own individual purpose.

I have only to look to my grandmother and mother for examples of breaking down barriers and leaving a legacy for me to follow. It is fairly reasonable to believe that many frowned upon my grandmother's marriage to my grandfather in 1948, her coming from a poor Irish-Catholic family and him from a more slightly affluent Pennsylvania-Dutch (German) and French Protestant family. In order to marry, my grandmother was required to convert to his religion— essentially turning away from her family's deep-rooted religion and cultural identity.

Likewise, when my unwed teenage mother became pregnant with a black baby in 1969, I doubt any would have described her pregnancy as a "good" thing. Many voiced their anger at my mother and my grandmother; several demonstrated their anger through the burning of crosses on their lawn, verbal abuse, and physical threats.

As a result of my mother's and grandmother's decisions, they were forced to live outside the social "norms" of their time. In essence, they redefined their values, and changed their views on how people were expected to behave. By going against their family's traditions, expectations, and approval, they broke down barriers that had consistently told them what was right or wrong, good or bad.

Following in my mother's and grandmother's footsteps, I too became more open to new types of relationships once I removed my own personal barriers and sought to live a more conscious life. My marriage is a testament to this, as my husband and I have almost every conceivable difference: age, race, nationality, educational background, and economic status.

Cost of Expectations

We create expectations for ourselves, live up to them or don't, use them as a standard of measurement, hold them over others, and fervently rebel against them. No matter the source of the expectation, the weightless words carry a heavy burden.

We create expectations when we attempt to exercise control over our lives by defining an intended outcome. Stemming from our judgments, expectations may define what we believe we (and others) can reasonably achieve, or they may characterize a set of behaviors by which we (and others) are to live by.

Unlike hope, which does not place a high level of certainty on an outcome, and so we are more willing to accept an outcome that is different from what we had hoped, expectations, on the other hand, come with a high level of certainty and desire for a specific outcome. Therefore, the holder of the expectation is less likely to accept an outcome other than the one expected.

This is one of life's few "golden nuggets": to become flexible enough to accept outcomes other than those we had hoped, expected, or planned. We must be willing to bend with the winds of change, amid happiness, pain, joy, and sorrow. Change is the essence of life. The more we adapt to change, the less of a struggle life may feel, and the greater our feeling of being content and fulfilled.

Freedom from Right or Wrong

Freeing ourselves from the concepts of right or wrong, good or bad, is not a license to live or act without good judgment—that is similar to giving someone permission to "throw the baby out with the bathwater." Rather, it is important to accept and recognize that our actions have consequences, and that those consequences may be harmful to ourselves and others.

Rather, I am proposing that we get rid of the bathwater—the defined substance floating around us: inherited and learned values, expectations, principles, and other constraints keeping us from making unbiased, conscious decisions that we can live with—but keep the baby—that which is most important: the cumulative learning from our personal life experiences.

Many would agree that having an addiction to alcohol is a bad choice. I would say, instead, it is not a conscious choice, and could be potentially harmful, and therefore, may not be in a person's best interest. However, I would also argue that if the alcoholic were to overcome their addiction to alcohol, and as a result, discover a life-affirming passion, then the line between right or wrong, good or bad, or what's in a person's best interest, becomes blurred.

What is in our best interest is to use each experience (whether others deem the experience right or wrong, good or bad) as a learning tool to help us overcome fears, break down barriers, and create opportunities in our lives. That's the whole point of jumping!

What decision, if any, have you made because you thought it was the "right" thing to do? Was it what you wanted? Have you ever made a decision to do something that others thought was "wrong" but it felt like the "right" thing to do? How did it make you feel going against others' expectations? Can you think of a time when a loved one made a choice other than what you had hoped or expected? Do you believe you have made conscious decisions most of the time?

Step 3 – Shit or Get off the Pot

Unlike my grandmother's other sayings, this one was a relatively later addition to her repertoire. Because of this, it is not laden with painful stories as the others were. Fortunately, I can remember her saying the words. Unfortunately, I can no longer remember the specific occasions that gave rise to the words, or who they were intentionally directed towards. Whether it was because I too had grown immune to her voice, or that my capacity for storing painful memories had reached its lifetime capacity, it saddens me in any case. We may do our best to keep our loved one's memories alive in our hearts and minds, but time has a way of fading those memories, surely and steadily, sometimes even against our will.

All is not lost. I have preserved these words in a mindful time capsule with the others, using them as a tool all the same. But before we go any further, however, I fear I may have not been completely honest thus far. It has not been my intention to misrepresent the facts, so much as it has been important that we are clear about the principles (especially for this last step: to do what others may see as the impossible—jump). While I have taken my grandmother's words to heart, and shared difficult stories within these pages, I have purposefully chosen to express the lessons in a positive light by focusing on the learnings, rather than the harsh realities and circumstances that had occurred that brought forth the words from my grandmother's mouth.

But I find that with this step, "Shit or Get off the Pot," I am all out of positive light. The reality was that my last few years living at home were the most difficult of my entire life, which also heartbreakingly coincided with my grandmother's last living years. By the time my grandmother adopted this new saying, she was tired, her body was worn down (from the heaviness of holding up a dependent family), and she was physically suffering from years of chain smoking.

I can only assume that her spirit was fueled only by the flickering light of the dying embers of unfulfilled hopes and past happiness, leaving less light to shine on her family. In my heart, she will always be a beacon of hope for me, but the reality was, at this stage in her life, she was mostly bitter, angry, and filled with resentment.

So when I hear these words particularly, I have no story to assign to them, no happy ending to attribute to them. All I am left with is the feeling of the resigned desperation in her voice when she said: "Shit or get off the pot."

In retrospect, I am fairly confident that my grandmother said this to lash out at us for hurting her—constantly letting her down, not living up to her expectations—even me, her miracle child, who screwed up on many occasions—and to remind us of what we could not, or would not, do to help ourselves. Essentially, by her words, she was threateningly saying to us: If you don't have what it takes to get the job done, then get the hell out of my way so I can do it for you.

That's how she was, and in many ways how I can be, when I'm not careful or conscious of my own thoughts and actions. I have the same natural tendencies as my grandmother, particularly when it comes to my dominating, overbearing, overprotective ways with my mother and my daughter. Thankfully, my husband is my anchor, often stopping me in my tracks when I try to have it on with him. Every once in a while, I find myself unconsciously stepping into my grandmother's shoes. Luckily, she was a size 8 and I'm only a 7!

Unlike the other expressions, this one had partially revealed its deeper meaning to me years before I began this journey of discovery. Yet, it stood alone, dangling in the winds of life, detached from the other lessons, so it did not have the same impact as it later would.

The Last Piece of the Puzzle

When I awoke the morning after hearing my grandmother's encouraging, dreamland advice, telling me to open my eyes and get on with living, the satisfaction and relief was incredible. A watershed moment occurred when I realized I had already been holding the last piece of the puzzle for many years and had never realized it. Imagine my excitement, which was not too dissimilar to putting together a large puzzle.

Growing up in the 70s, puzzles were a major part of my childhood. Whether they were set up on a metal TV stand, or on a living room coffee table, or because of their size and complexity, held a more prominent place, such as on a dining room table, there were always puzzles waiting to be solved—at my Grandmother Rita's house, at her siblings' homes, at my other grandmother's house, at cousins' and friends' homes. Solving puzzles was an integral part of everyday life, before cable television and the internet infiltrated our homes and minds.

We'd scratch our heads, pick up pieces to identify and catalogue their unique characteristics, stare at one piece for what seemed like an eternity, and then put it down, only to do the same with another piece. After pre-sorting the pieces by color and edge direction, there was always the one that didn't fit in with the rest—its shape, size, and color were so different that it didn't match up to any others. For the sake of time, it would be set aside, to be dealt with later.

Then all of a sudden that ah-ha moment would occur—where the mind was finally able to work through its limited perception, and without hesitation could immediately see exactly where the odd piece fit into the picture. We then asked ourselves: *How could I not have seen that before?* The answer was staring us right in the face. It was so simple.

Like the last piece of the puzzle, separated and detached, the saying has less meaning, but when connected to the other pieces, it makes all the sense in the world.

The last lesson—which connects my grandmother's other lessons—involves timing: knowing when to act *and* when *not* to act, or putting it into context with my grandmother's words: *knowing when to shit and when to get off the pot.* Timing is the glue that holds the vision and the decision to jump together. Without the right timing, no matter how clear we are with our vision or that we're making the *right* decision, our plans are less likely to be successful if it is not at the right *time*.

When is it the Right Time? And What do the Greeks have to do with it?

The matter of time is a subject very dear to my heart, and one that is a constant point of contention between my husband and myself. Time has always played a critical part in our relationship, living between two continents and having a five-hour difference in time for fifteen years. We needed to be absolutely clear when considering time, whether it was to schedule a phone call, make an appointment, or just to be able to relate to each other, since our time was mismatched—I was often home from work at the same time that he was going to bed. The friction between us lies in the fact that we have extremely opposite approaches to how we think about time.

To illustrate our fundamental differences, my husband wears a watch—which I've lovingly nicknamed the "Rolodex"—about 18-20 hours a day. It is one of the first things he puts on in the morning, and the last thing he takes off at night, and the object of many searches when he's taken it off in unusual places. In addition to his "Rolodex," he has any number of other watches with special purposes and holders that he wears depending on the activity.

As for myself, I can only remember owning four watches in my entire life: a Mickey Mouse one I had growing up in the 70s, a Swatch finger one with interchangeable colored bands to look cool in the 80s, a Timex that my sister-in-law bought me for my first professional job interview in the 90s, and a Virgin Atlantic dual time zone watch that my husband gave me shortly after we met to help me easily calculate our time difference.

Sometimes we are able to laugh about our different approaches; however, more often than not, our differences have been the cause of more arguments in our relationship than any other issue. For my husband (and I should also add my daughter), the notion of time is largely the structure that keeps life in order. It is the vessel into which the uncertainty of life may be contained, giving one a sense of assurance. It is to be measured precisely, exactly, and never estimated.

Not surprising then that, unlike my husband and daughter, I am always late, even when I try my hardest not to be late. Without sounding like a victim, it seems that no matter what I do, something always "jinxes" me, causing me to be late. My husband has given my problem, which causes this phenomena to occur, a name: "time and task dyslexia." Now, whenever I am late, I simply remind him of my condition.

Putting jokes aside, the heart of the matter is that I am fundamentally against using measured time as a basis for making life decisions, whether it is measured on a calendar or a clock, and I feel very uncomfortable and constrained when doing so. To me, the thought of wearing a watch is a lot like how Gollum felt when Frodo put the string-like leash around Gollum's neck: he gagged, choked, and kept falling over, unable to walk straight. Something deep within me intensely dislikes the idea of trying to fit life between the numbers of a clock.

In my defense, however, and thanks to my husband, I completely understand that my philosophical approach to time can, and sometimes does, impact others—so I work really hard to respect others by being on time for appointments and when fulfilling obligations and commitments made to others.

In discussing my and my husband's time problem with a friend in our retail store, he asked me: "Have you heard of the two Greek words for "time"?" He explained that the

Ancient Greeks actually had two words to describe time, and while most of us are familiar with the first word, *chronos*, as in chronology, he said few people were aware of the other word to describe time: *kairos*.

The impact of his words, when he explained kairos to me, pierced through my layers of misunderstanding and ignorance, igniting a revelation that has since become an integral element of my own understanding of myself. Suddenly, it all began to make sense.

Kairos refers to the *right* time or a *perfect* time, a time not measured in seconds, minutes, hours, or days, but an *opportune* time to act. And since it cannot be measured, it cannot be planned—rather, it is felt and sensed. It is interconnected with all other things, requiring us to keep a watchful eye on events happening around us, then making an assessment as to how the events relate to us and how they may benefit us.

Timing and Keeping Time

Being a kairos-based person living with two chronos-based people can be very challenging to say the least. Because we are on opposite ends of the time spectrum, my husband, daughter, and I frequently have heated debates. Most of the time, I find myself on the losing side, because I am *always* outnumbered two-to-one.

I can't say that I like their approaches, but I can say that I value and appreciate their perspectives. They have taught me an important life lesson, another proverbial "golden nugget": valuing and respecting both types of time, the right time and the actual time, gives us the best chance of success, no matter what tasks we undertake, but most importantly when we jump. Let me explain…

Once we have created our vision (Step 1) and made the final decision to jump (Step 2), the last step is to act (Step 3)—in other words: jump.

The timing of our jump is just as important as the previous steps of creating our vision and making the decision.

In order to give ourselves the best chance of walking away after landing, we must be emotionally, mentally, physically, and spiritually prepared to jump. This can be almost impossible to do when we are under extreme stress when making our way to the cliff's edge.

How can we prepare ourselves if we are so stressed out from our current situation? When will we know the right time to jump?

I cannot answer these questions, as we alone must find the answers that we seek, and seeking them is part of our individual journey, as well as taking responsibility for choosing the right time to jump. What I can say is, we can increase our chances of success by striking a balance between finding the right time to jump and managing our time—in essence, understanding and mastering both types of time: kairos and chronos.

We should allow ourselves to take comfort in the fact that we have made it to Step 3. Provided that we are aware of these steps, we may begin to let go of the things that are holding us back: our anxiety, worry, and stress that is associated with the continual stirrings of unknown, unmet, unfulfilled needs and desires (Step 1); and the sleepless nights, anguish, and agony associated with making the final decision to jump (Step 2).

Imagine this as a rest stop along the path to the cliff's edge— another "breather" to rest our weary feet and souls. Having this momentary break creates the space that our minds need to imagine creative solutions, where all things are possible— at the *right* time. We free ourselves from the limited perception of our vantage point—much like solving a puzzle—then we are able to clearly see how the pieces fit together and to decide when is the best time for us to jump. This is *kairos* time.

But the *kairos* approach to time only gives us half the story. Skillfully mastering our *chronos* time further supports our progress, by increasing the likelihood of following through the opening created by *kairos*. If you are like me and find it difficult to fit life between the numbers of a clock or a calendar, find solace in the fact that by doing so, we are much more productive and efficient with our time. And in times of great change, our workloads and pressures seem to escalate, demanding more from us than life would normally ask. So it goes without saying then, that being productive with our time can, and will, ease the stress and strains of a life affected by major change.

Creating a monthly calendar, weekly goals, daily tasks, and tracking our progress (at the start and the end of each day) are tools we can employ to increase our productivity.

Often intentionally personified as Father Time and the Grim Reaper, the Greeks do caution us to remain mindful of *chronos*. They remind us that keeping track of time can be a daunting and draining task, and if we get too sucked into the "keeping of time," we are liable to lose sight of *kairos* and our perspective (the proverbial "wood for the trees"). *Chronos* time has a way of "sucking the joy" out of living.

So we must try to find a balance between the two—kairos and chronos—to achieve the most peace and productivity in life.

What is your natural approach with regard to time? Would you say you are more kairos- or chronos-oriented? How comfortable are you when plans that affect you change? Can you think of any occasions when you needed to change your plans, because it did not feel like the right time? On a scale of 1 to 10, how do you rate your level of productivity? What can you do to be more efficient?

Pushing Will Only Cause More Pain

During our three-year wait for the *right* time to move to England, I began to slowly make the connection between my grandmother's saying and the concept of the *right* time, which reassured me tremendously.

When we had made the decision to move, three years prior to the move, we painfully faced the reality of our situation: We were completely exhausted from maintaining the retail business, with no fuel left in our souls to overcome our exhaustion; my husband was increasingly desiring to be closer to his growing family in England; I had a growing list of minor health issues, which was becoming a major issue, because of the long-term lack of healthcare as a small business owner; and lastly, we were financially drowning from the high cost of living in one of America's richest states during *The Great Recession.*

Unknowingly, we progressed through Step 1: we created a vision and eliminated barriers. The vision relied on the safety net of a fully paid home and a national healthcare system, where one's health did not have to suffer or be determined by one's career choices.

But most importantly, we knew the move would allow my husband and me to be there for our children. We could cherish raising my husband's grandchildren, while, at the same time, providing my daughter with financial support to attend university—something we could not do in our current situation.

We began to explore options to sell the house and tie up financial loose ends. With no tangible plan in hand, other than a somewhat romanticized vision of British life, and a growing awareness that we were drowning in a sinking ship, we were still uncertain as to how it would all work.

Even though we inadvertently accomplished Step 1 (created a vision and eliminated barriers), we were acutely aware that we had to make a decision—Step 2. A jump of this size and magnitude would not happen otherwise, not unless we made it happen. Slowly, we settled into a final decision.

Tide and Time Wait for No Man

Just as our plans began to take shape, out of the blue, I learned of a job vacancy as a Business Advisor. I was reluctant at first to pursue it. In my mind, it would require me to "give up" on dreams that I had for my business. I had no plans to close the business, but I knew in my heart that not being there day-to-day, in reality, meant I would be physically and mentally elsewhere. When I told my husband and daughter about the job, they both immediately saw only benefits, and, shall I say, strongly encouraged me to apply.

This is how the path to the cliff's edge is: One day, the path forward is clear and straight-forward; the next day, we may be led through a maze of densely wooded forest, taking away not only our sense of direction, but making it nearly impossible to see our way forward.

Now as an employee once again—and not just an employer—many of our problems disappeared overnight: my daughter and I had a solid healthcare plan; there was a steady flow of money deposited into the bank, money that arrived without me having to put it there in the first place; and my husband was able to sleep better at night.

We refinanced into a longer-term mortgage, loosening the high mortgage noose that was tightening around our necks. Pleased that our original 15-year mortgage saved us from going "under water," enabling us to pay off more of our original mortgage—at a time when many homeowners owed more on their homes than their homes were worth—we could now breathe a bit easier knowing we could pay the new lower mortgage.

Life was stable for the moment. So we rested amongst the green, healing foliage along the cliff's edge. By setting aside our plans to move, as my grandmother would say, *we got off the pot.* While our plans were not forgotten, they were out of our minds, allowing us to fully rest and recharge.

We did not push or strain against the tides of change, which would have only caused us more pain and anguish. We let nature take its course, so to speak, knowing that if it was meant to be, it would be. While we were clueless as to what was happening, it was clearly *not* the right time to jump.

Dropping Weight, Traveling Light

The fires that fueled our passions were dimming under the grueling seven-days-a-week work schedule I had maintained for over a year to keep both the business and the job. With the new healthcare and a new lease on life, I received physical therapy for an old injury, which I could not otherwise get without healthcare. I discovered through regular check-ups that, at only forty years old, I was rapidly collecting health issues as if I'd been playing "Pick Up Sticks": high blood pressure, a second fibroid, an even larger uterus, no longer twenty but fifty pounds overweight, and was, once again, well down the road to full-blown diabetes—having had gestational diabetes during my pregnancy, which required insulin injections two to three times a day.

It was now time to let go of our plans to jump, and fully recharge. Starting with the extra fat I'd been carrying, I lost forty pounds and had a minor gynecological surgery.

The physical strength I gained from the weight loss, and from no longer being anemic, gave me the courage to let go of living the American dream through business ownership. After announcing plans to close the store, we were fortunate to find a buyer to pick up the fair trade torch. Lastly, we embarked on ten years' worth of home repairs that the demands of the business had kept us from undertaking.

Two years passed, and we were still resting, recharging, and *off the pot*. While we postponed the jump, we did not forget about our long-term vision (Step 1), nor the decision (Step 2) we had painstakingly made. Our plan to jump was always there in the back of our minds, waiting like a coiled snake for the *right* time. It was clear to us that this was only a temporary rest stop. What was not clear was for how long.

Six months after selling the business, I was laid off from the job, and with that single change, we knew it was time to gather up our belongings and, once again, get back on the path towards the cliff's edge. The last stretch would be treacherous, without a doubt, and would take all of our strength. It would be another twelve months before we finally made it to the edge, as we still had to get our UK visas, finish the necessary house repairs, prepare the house for selling, and sell off most of our physical possessions, as we decided to jump light—essentially, make a clean break.

All in all, it would take us 36 months from the time that we made the decision to jump (Step 2) until we actually jumped (Step 3). We could not have anticipated the prolonged rest period, nor foresaw the hurdles we would face—before and after jumping.

Through it all, however, my grandmother's words stayed by my side, comforting me, by providing a beacon of hope— something they had failed to do while she was still alive.

Do you believe there is a right time to act? How do you know when that time is? Have you postponed taking action because it did not feel like the right time? What did you do while you waited? What is the longest you have waited to act? What did you do to keep your dream alive while you waited? Did you ever give up because the wait seemed too long? How long is too long?

CHAPTER 5

LET'S JUMP

You Gotta Jump!

Steve Harvey

Getting Ready

Words cannot express the heightened sense of fear we may experience when we finally arrive at the cliff's edge. When we take those last few steps forward, and align the tops of our toes with the last morsels of earth, this seemingly small act—quoting my grandmother—is enough to "scare the shit out of you."

Nothing can prepare us for the experience. Nothing. No amount of rationalizing what we think we're going to think will prepare us, neither will trying to anticipate how we're going to feel when we face the "wall of fear." I call it the wall of fear, because in that moment, there is nothing beyond that wall—no earth to stand on, no person to lean on, no excuses left to tell ourselves. All that is left is ourselves and our fears.

Jumping is a singularly solitary act. We are alone with our lone feelings. And while others may experience it with us, have gone before us, or have experienced similar situations as us, no two jumps will ever be the same. Our fears are ours to own and unique to us, filtered through our lens of life at that particular moment in time.

Is it Really Jumping if it's All in Our Heads? Physical versus Mental Jumps.

Central to our preparations for jumping is determining the type of jump we will make. Knowing the type of jump, *before* our feet leave the cliff's edge, can facilitate a safer landing by helping us to stay grounded and accept the outcome after jumping (we'll discuss this further in Chapter 6: "Landing Safely").

Will we be making a change to our physical surroundings, with say a new job, house, or town? Perhaps, we will be ending a relationship and living alone for the first time in many years.

Alternatively, our jump may not produce any physical changes to our day-to-day lives, but instead result in a change within ourselves, in essence, changing the way we think about something or how we act when something happens.

The previous examples illustrate the two types of jumps we can make: physical and mental jumps.

Let's take a closer look, starting with the latter: mental jumps. It may be easy to think, *If nothing in our lives has changed, except our thinking, have we really jumped?* My answer would be a super big *YES*—without a doubt!

These types of jumps can be the most profound and fundamentally life-changing than any physical jump. Mental jumps occur when we permanently shift our thinking, make a final decision, or learn to accept external situations that are outside of our control.

They may include: living life with passion, living each day as if it were our last, putting our health and wellbeing first, losing weight, learning to live addiction-free, reducing stress, changing parenting styles for the betterment of our children, spending more time with our families, letting go of expectations that we set for ourselves and others, coming to terms with things that we have no control over (for example, not getting the promotion we had hoped to get, not having more money, not finding a loving partner, not having children), shifting our focus away from ourselves by dedicating our lives to helping others, and the most important of all mental jumps, *loving ourselves unconditionally for who we are*. As you can see, the list is potentially endless.

Since mental jumps do not cause an *immediate* physical change to our day-to-day lives, our lives may look the same *before* and *after* jumping, deceiving us into believing we had not jumped. Fundamentally, our everyday lives consist of the same life-building blocks: we wake in the morning; get dressed; plan our day; prepare meals; take care of things, ourselves, our children, parents, neighbors; exercise; go to work; read; watch television; do a hobby—all before going to bed, only to do it again the next day.

While it may seem that life is the same after a mental jump, as we go about moving from one life block to another, and from one day to another, however, inside we are different. We are *thinking* differently, which over time may result in subtle changes to our physical landscape. We may see that our belt is looser around our waist as a result of taking our lunch into work instead of ordering fast food. Or we become motivated to finish a house project that we've been putting off, because we have more energy as a result of not having a beer or two after work. Lastly, we may begin to find peace with a painful reality, such as accepting the possibility that we may not find a loving partner—allowing us to experience love through other types of relationships.

Like that slow, intermittent drip of change, our thinking, perceptions, feelings, emotions, and judgments may have been continually shifting, evolving over a long period of time, slowly leading us to the cliff's edge. We may have already experienced many false jumps along the path to the cliff's edge. A good example is when people *try* to quit smoking, before finally quitting. Like many, it took me many years of "trying to quit" before I finally quit. However long and slow the transition time, I strongly believe we will eventually arrive at our destination, where *trying* ends and *doing* begins—in other words, the mental cliff's edge.

Because of the uniquely evolving nature of mental jumps, occasionally we may have *unconsciously* began to think and act differently. It may even appear that we have already jumped. And while I'd love to say we have, this is not the case. The same principles apply here that we discussed earlier when we are pushed over the cliff's edge, rather than jumping. Since jumping requires us to make a conscious decision, and while our thinking and behaviors may have already changed, it is only when we have consciously acknowledged those changes within ourselves that we have made a mental jump.

Contrary to mental jumps, a physical jump gives rise to *immediate* physical changes in our day-to-day lives. For example, physical jumps may include: changing jobs; relocating to a new city for love, a new job, adventure; starting a business; adopting or birthing a new life; moving— as a result of separation or a divorce; quitting a job to care for a loved one; dealing with life changes as a result of a sudden onset of a debilitating health issue and heartbreakingly, the loss of a child, parent, life partner, or spouse.

Under these circumstances, when we land after these types of jumps, there is no mistaking that life is vastly different. Our physical landscape has changed, and with this change we may have also suffered a trauma, or are filled with excitement—depending on the nature of the jump.

Physical jumps, while more obvious on the surface, are not necessarily easier or harder than mental jumps—just different. Each jump comes with its own set of challenges and considerations. One type of jump can facilitate the other. Similar to hope and courage, a mental jump may, in fact, lead to a physical jump, and vice-versa.

Reality Check

We must be absolutely clear about some things before we jump. We should consider the following questions before jumping:

Can we clearly articulate the nature of the jump? What is the life-changing act we are undertaking: quitting a job, starting a business, getting married, getting a divorce, having a child, deciding not to have a child, learning to live addiction-free, dealing with a life-threatening health issue?

When we strip the reasons for jumping down to its barest form, we have clarity. Having this moment of clarity before our jump gives us one last chance for the proverbial "reality check," and if needed, to change our minds.

Changing our mind is not a sign of weakness, nor is it a "bad" thing. It takes courage to choose another option after we've decided on a course of action, because in some cases, it requires us to admit that we may have been wrong. If this is the case, it may take more courage to change our mind than to follow through with a decision that we know is not in our best interest. By shifting our perspective about changing our minds after we've made a decision, we may then see it as an act of self-love.

With a firm decision to jump in hand, it is important to clearly articulate what the jump represents to us in our lives: Why are we doing it? Have we faced our fears, vetted our reasons? Are we clear about how our jump may affect our loved ones? Do we have a crystal clear vision of what we hope to achieve after the jump? Do we trust our beliefs? Recognizing that our life will be different after the jump, and possibly different than what we anticipated, expected, hoped, do we have a plan for landing? Do we have a what-if or worst case scenario plan? Do we have an "out" strategy, in the case of an extreme emergency?

Imagery and metaphors can help us to deal with the intense fear and physical stress our bodies may experience before the jump, but when all is said and done, *we must jump with absolute clarity*, whether we jump with open or closed eyes! We must clearly understand the actions we are taking, the potential consequences, and be willing to accept responsibility for those actions and consequences. If we have done this upfront work, we will gain strength through our jump. If we have not, we risk becoming victims after we land.

Can you visualize your jump? How high is the cliff? Can you see your wall of fear? What is your wall of fear telling you? Are you absolutely clear about your reasons for jumping? Are you at peace with your decision? Are you ready?

Trusting in Ourselves

Metaphorically speaking, how we go over the edge is our choice. For me personally, each jump has been uniquely different. One jump, I excitedly kept my eyes wide open, felt the thrill of exhilaration when my feet left the ground, and had an overall sense that I would be "alright"—no matter what. In actuality, it was more akin to flying than jumping. Perhaps this was because I could see what I was getting into, liked what I saw, and had abundant confidence.

This last jump, however, was the complete opposite. It was as if I were standing at the edge of the cliff blind-folded in the dark, with a thick, cold mist blanketing me. One single unknown factor held the key to my and my family's future life: our UK visas. We anxiously waited, day after day, with our future lives hanging in anticipation for them to arrive.

Would we be denied visas? How would we cope with being denied? How long would we have to wait to find out? Six weeks, twelve weeks, or six months? Would we receive them before my daughter started university? What if we sold the house before finding out? Then, without a home or a job, what would we do if we were denied visas? How long would our marriage last if we couldn't move? If the house didn't sell, how long could we afford to pay the mortgage on it after we had moved? To say the very least, these lingering unknown questions made it impossible to see the cliff's edge.

Besides facing the wall of fear in complete darkness, unable to gauge the height at which we stood, I could not see how far the distance was to the bottom of the cliff. That distance, which determined the size of the jump, was largely dependent on a variety of interconnected unknowns: the approval of our UK visas, the timing of selling the house, the final selling price, my daughter's university applications, receiving a job offer before receiving our visas, and lastly, my cat's pet passport—how would I cope without my Zen Master?

With all the comings and goings of my daughter, who spent weekends and holidays with her father; my husband, who divided his time between two countries; and my parents, who lived 500 miles away, like her feline predecessor before her, the "Protector," Zen Master, was the only constant in my chaotic on-again-off-again family life.

Nearly all was unknown to me, except for the deep trust I had in myself and my life's purpose. Cutting through the dense wall of fear, this knowledge provided me the strength that I needed to jump, regardless of when the jump would happen or how big of a jump it would be.

On the surface, I was dealing with these issues every waking minute, but when I laid my head down at the end of the night, it was trust and the desire to live my life's purpose that provided me a deep sense of peace, allowing me to sleep. I will not lie, some days were harder than others not to crack under the pressure. Some days, the extreme stress would cause an eruption of tears at any moment, which I just let flow—accompanied by a glass or two of wine.

While my mind was clouded with fear, my trust was unaffected. I believe this is because I'd vetted my reasons for jumping. I knew why I was *not* jumping, and why I *was* jumping. I was not jumping out of fear. I was not jumping to run away from someone or a situation. Yes, the situation was difficult, but I knew I could "make it" if we stayed in the States.

I was choosing not to just "make it." I was choosing to live my life's purpose. I wasn't trying to be someone other than who I was, or moving to England because I thought I was better than anyone else.

I didn't have romantic Anglophile notions of life based on Downton Abbey, Foyle's War, or Bridget Jones' Diary. Oddly, the opposite was true. Our standard of living in England would be simpler, less materially focused. While we would be comfortable, we knew we would be living with a lot less material "things" and "mod cons" than we had in the States.

Ironically, for this reason, I always felt more like *me* in England, the whole me: the *black* me and the *white* me. Unlike the disconnected lives that I lived in the States—twenty-plus years in a deprived black world with a healthy dose of drugs, violence, and racism, followed by twenty years in an upper-middle class white world, filled with too many comforts, leading me to have a healthy dose of unrealistic expectations and a sense of entitlement that I guiltily fought not to feel— I would have a more integrated, realistic life in the UK.

A life that balanced needs and wants, while keeping rampant consumerism at bay. I would enjoy the larger-than-life, "big" feeling of living in England—with its appreciation for history, exploration, travel, and ethnically-diverse foods of the former empire—yet live and work on a "small" island, where I'd struggle daily to find "extra" space and feel pride in having less.

At the end of the day, I knew in my heart that I was jumping for love—for both myself and my family. I relied on the sixteen years of deep peace and serenity that I felt whenever

I spent time in England, and the heaviness I felt upon returning to the States. I relied on the sense that I was going home rather than leaving home. This profound sense of trust told me it was time to take care of me; the weariness of life was too much and I needed to rest.

More than anything, I believed it was the compassionate thing to do for my husband, as he had carried the burden of travel for those sixteen years. His restless nights checking and re-checking his endless to do lists, and keeping up two homes in two continents, was becoming too much for him to bear alone.

Along these same lines, I needed to be more settled for my daughter, so that she too would be better prepared for the challenges of university and adult life. My grandmother's stable life provided me the anchor I needed to launch into adulthood. And I needed to do the same for my daughter— to be her anchor during these important transitional years. Living in England with a modicum of financial security would allow me to stop scrambling from job to job, while trying to prop up an unsustainable, materially-wealthy life.

The financial strains, and ten years of business ownership, had taken a toll on my relationship with my daughter, leading her to believe she always came second to the business, and the business, to her, was like having "a delinquent older brother"—always in trouble, always getting the attention.

Lastly, my heart was telling me it was time to focus on my mother, whose health had continued to deteriorate. By having a simpler, less materially-focused and stressful life, I believed I would be able to be there for her, *really* there, not just physically present, and *there* for me and my family.

Have you had to make a difficult decision that required a profound trust in yourself? What did you do to build confidence in your belief in yourself to make the decision? How did you feel prior to making the decision and afterwards? Would you make the same decision again?

Take a Deep Breath and…Jump!

That's all there is to it. It is often the mental anguish that we put ourselves through that makes it so difficult. The reality is, we walk up to the cliff's edge and jump. We can get a running start, or we can simply step off the edge. We may keep our eyes open or closed. We can hold our breath, or scream at the top of our lungs. We can do whatever we choose, as long as we acknowledge the process and own what is happening.

We have made a decision and acted on that decision, despite the intense fear. We are hopeful that life will be better; we are confident that the change will enable us to address unfulfilled needs; we believe in ourselves, as we are; and we are prepared to accept responsibility—no matter the outcome.

We take a deep breath.

Then we jump.

CHAPTER 6

LANDING SAFELY

*If you talk to the animals they will talk with you
and you will know each other. If you do not talk to them
you will not know them, and what you do not know
you will fear. What one fears one destroys.*

Chief Dan George

Getting Up

At some point after jumping we will land. The sensation of freefalling is replaced with an increasing awareness that our feet are once again on solid ground. We slowly become cognizant of our new landscape, which varies depending on the height of the cliff and intensity of our fears. Life may appear comfortably familiar, giving us a modicum of security while presenting us with reasonably challenging new situations to overcome, or it may appear completely foreign, taking away any sense of security, pushing us to the outer limits of our comfort zone.

Regardless of how comfortable or foreign our new lives may appear after landing, or the type of jump we've made (mental or physical), we will need to get up and take stock of our new lives. Getting up is about standing up, and if needed, healing our injuries from landing. It requires us to face our new and old fears with the intention of overcoming them (explained in the upcoming section called, *Getting Over*), so that we walk away from the landing site in a position of power: self-empowered.

Getting up says, "Great, now that you've landed, what are you going to do?"

Landing after a Mental Jump: Staying Grounded

After landing from a mental jump, life may deceivingly look the same as it did the day before. Herein lies the greatest challenge with mental jumps: We may be fooled into thinking that we have not jumped, as it is far too easy to go back, because "back" is within the realm of our thinking.

How we stop ourselves from going back is an individual choice and it is our responsibility to do so. If we do not take responsibility for our actions, after we land, we risk going back and becoming victims. Should we accept responsibility for our actions, we have landed in a position of power; then it is easier to continue the course. Knowing that we have jumped is critical to our success, and is equally important as facing our fears in our new reality.

Fully committing ourselves 100% to the belief that we have jumped and landed will create a new script in our belief system that will provide us with the strength and courage needed to keep our feet on solid ground after landing—in other words, to stay grounded.

Prior to jumping, we created a vision of what life should look like after the jump, and eliminated those things that were holding us back from that vision. But now that we've landed, what does it look, feel, seem, and even taste like? Does the day after we jumped look brighter, knowing that the dark clouds that were hovering over us are now gone? Does sex feel better, knowing that we have accepted ourselves for who we are? Does it feel easier to turn away from bad eating choices? Does food taste better without the residue of tobacco in our mouth?

Is life how we envisioned, or better than we anticipated? What changes have surprised us that we could not have anticipated? How have our basic building blocks of life changed since landing? Has our daily routine changed since landing?

Modifying routines helps us to accept and incorporate our new reality into our lives. Driving a different way home from work, instead of passing our favorite "happy hour" spot, may make it easier to go straight home. Packing a lunch, instead of ordering out, makes it easier to control our cravings. Leaving ourselves notes, reminding us of the benefits of our decision, can help keep it fresh in our mind when we find it hard to stay the course.

While adjustments to our daily routine may give us an advantage, ultimately, we must overcome the problem that led us to jump in the first place. How we do this is personal to each individual and each jump. There is no shortcutting this process. We must be diligent. Perhaps knowing that it may take several years to fully overcome the challenge, with ups and downs occurring when we encounter our fears and past issues in different situations, is all part of the process. This realization may give us support over the long course. And reminding ourselves of what we've gained from jumping—and not what we've lost—may help keep us grounded after landing.

No Baby on Board

The single hardest decision I have made was when I let go of my dream of having a second child—a child with my then-life partner, now my husband.

When my husband and I met, I was a recently separated 28-year-old mother of a three-year-old, living hundreds of miles from any family member. Each day was a struggle. Although I had a well-paying job, I barely had money for food, because of the financial entanglements of a separation, not to mention my constant stomach pains caused by the emotional stress from the separation, and my constant worry about how it was affecting my daughter—whom I love with all my heart and soul.

My daughter's father and I both held demanding jobs, but without our large supportive families to help us that we both had growing up. Therefore, we were solely dependent on each other to raise our daughter. For these reasons, on every level—emotionally, mentally, and financially—having another child was the farthest thought from my mind at the time. My sole focus was caring for my daughter. I simply could not imagine having another child.

Unlike me, my now-husband's three children were well on their way to full adulthood when we met, and he was just stepping into his fifties. Having another child was not on his to-do list either, to say the least. The matter was not an issue, because we were in agreement.

Five years later, we were living a sanitized, poorer version of *Pretty Woman*. Life was truly a fairy tale, with romance, exotic travel, and adventure. We thoroughly enjoyed each other and so we decided to further combine our independent lives. After my husband was unexpectedly offered an early retirement, we bought our dream suburban family home with a whirlpool bathtub, fenced-in yard, and within walking distance to downtown Mystic. My daughter was feeling more settled and was making new friends. It was a golden time for her and me as well. We began taking mother-daughter weekend trips to New York and Boston as she transformed from a toddler into a "little buddy."

Amongst the tall blades of happiness, a dark awareness was lurking in the distance, causing an unknown stirring deep within me. Unbeknownst to me, it slowly began to unfurl itself.

I was aware of being out-of-sync with peers of my age, but the gap between us was widening as they became bogged down with morning sickness and changing diapers. Having my daughter at a younger age than my co-workers who were my age, they were now having their first child when mine was quickly becoming a preadolescent.

My daughter's school friends all had younger siblings, or their parents were having their second and third children. Now in my mid-thirties, my biological clock was ringing louder than ever, and unrealistically feeling like Cinderella, I wanted more than anything to have another child before the clock struck twelve. Unfortunately, my own desires were not enough to change my husband's mind.

At that time, every fiber of my being began to feel incomplete, knowing that I would never experience the joys of creating a new life with my husband, and leaving my daughter to be raised as a lonely only child, like myself.

While it broke my husband's heart to see me suffer, he did his best to console me. Rationally, I knew I'd feel and do the same as my husband if the roles were reversed; therefore, I wholeheartedly respected his decision.

Nonetheless, it was an impossible conundrum. Sadly, the mind cannot dictate how the heart feels. The years ticked on, and my chances of having another child were slowly slipping through my fingers. This was especially hard for me, coming from an upbringing where a woman's pride was deeply rooted in the fathers of her children, and I was taught to wait for "Mr. Right." But now that I had him, I would never have his children.

Although I was not fully aware of the concept of jumping then, I still found myself standing at the cliff's edge. It was my first conscious life-changing mental jump. Seeing it clearly, I had two choices: either stay with my husband (knowing full well that I would never have his child or any other children), or leave the relationship (with the possibility of having someone else's child before my biological clock struck twelve).

I couldn't help thinking to myself: *No one really knows for sure what happened to Cinderella in regards to the "happily ever after" bit.* But I got a feeling that it wasn't quite happily ever after.

Sparing these pages the depressing details, I can say that I cried lakes, then rivers, then streams for many, many years, and avoided babies as much as possible! It was, by far, the hardest conscious decision I ever had to make.

Taking a quote from *The Life of Brian* to look "on the bright side of life," I made the choice to stay with my husband, as the love we shared was more important to me than the idea of future children. And with time, my heart healed and I fully accepted my choice.

Today, I can honestly say—with a fully open, loving heart— that I am happy with the choice I made and have not one iota of regret. From that experience, a whole new *me* emerged: stronger, confident, and, for the first time, with a firm awareness of purpose. Redefining the expectations I'd placed on myself, I shattered the notion that I was incomplete without another child.

I learned that it was much harder to create my own vision than to go along with society's notions of what is expected of a woman. After the tears stopped blurring my vision, I decided that I would do something with my life that really, truly mattered to me: becoming a kick-ass, socially responsible business woman.

Do you have unresolved issues in your life that would require a mental jump? What has been the hardest decision you have had to make that required a major shift in your thinking? What did you do to keep from going back on your decision? Did you fully accept the decision? What did you do to overcome your fears before making the decision? How many other difficult decisions have you struggled with, and what did you do differently in each situation?

Landing after a Physical Jump: Adapting to Our New Reality

Unlike mental jumps, there is no mistaking when we've made a physical jump—it will have an immediate impact on our lives. Because of this, there may often be very real, immediate physical consequences to jumping.

Similar to how a mental jump may facilitate a physical shift in our day-to-day lives, the key to landing after a physical jump is adapting to our new reality with a mental shift. Depending on the nature of the physical jump, we may need an additional healing period after the jump before we are able to shift our thinking. It may all sound a bit much to wrap our heads around.

To illustrate, say that you have been told your job is being relocated to another state, far from friends and family. You have only a few short weeks to decide to relocate or be laid off. However, due to personal reasons, you are unable to move. This leaves you little time to find a new job or develop alternative sources of income. Almost over night, your everyday life has instantly and drastically changed—one day you're going to work, the next day you're not.

Sadly, this happens to many people every day. Along with losing a job, financial stability, and a sense of security, we have suddenly lost our daily structure—the reason behind many of our day-to-day activities. We may no longer need to get up at a specific time or spend time driving or commuting to work; we may have lost our feeling of being productive, or the satisfaction we gain from doing work; we may no longer have to plan our meal times around work schedules; and lastly, we may no longer need to go to bed at a specific time.

Putting aside the financial fears that being laid off may have created, or the emotional injuries suffered as a result of being laid off, practically speaking, it is important for us to create mental structure for our daily life. Simplistically, we have to figure out what we're going to do with our time, and how we will use our time to our advantage.

This is the most fundamental premise behind landing after a physical jump: becoming aware of our new physical landscape and creating a conscious plan to deal with it.

Feeling Good, Feeling Bad, and Feeling Pain

It is suffice to say that there is an infinite number of reasons that necessitate a jump. In spite of that, it seems to me that there are only three broad landing types: landings that feel good, landings that feel bad, and landings that cause an unbearable amount of pain.

It is usually only after we land that we are able to determine the landing type—the proverbial "catch 22." We may never fully know or understand how something will affect us until we have experienced it firsthand. A good example of this is when we become a parent for the first time. Others may share their wisdom with us, and we may try to imagine how our life will change with the addition of a new life, but the reality is always different from how we imagined— sometimes drastically different.

To illustrate landings that may feel good or bad, consider, for example, what happens when you leave a "bad" job for a "good" job. Most of us would expect to feel better after landing, right? Excited, enthusiastic, and hopeful, you leave the seemingly bad job for your dream job.

After a few months, you discover that your new boss takes all the credit for your work, embarrasses you during meetings, and passes you up when assigning the better projects. You had thought this was a good opportunity and you had done your research, but now you feel worse than before, stuck in yet another dead-end job. How could you have been so wrong?

Consider this second scenario: You learn from company announcements that you will be laid off from a job you love. You dread being laid off, racked with worry that you are unable to eat or sleep, so you begin taking yoga classes in order to cope with the stress.

After three months of waiting for the layoff, you realize that you are very passionate about yoga. When you are finally laid off, you train to become a yoga instructor and set up your own yoga studio. You now can't imagine your life not doing the work that you truly love. You didn't expect that being laid off could change your life for the better. How could you have been so wrong?

There are some jumps, however, that are in a class of their own. This is the case when we must make a decision under extremely painful, emotional situations. These jumps typically stay with us for the rest of our lives as if they leave an imprint on our souls.

The final decision preceding the jump may be almost impossible to make, or may have life or death consequences; these include: making the decision to give a child up for adoption or have an abortion, because you see no other option; giving "do not resuscitate" orders for the person who means the most to you; or being pressured into making the decision to take an abusive loved one off of life support.

These types of decisions are potentially soul-destroying, as they can make us feel that the very core of our being will be destroyed if we make the "wrong" decision. With time, patience, acceptance, and an abundance of self love, we can, and do, heal after making these types of jumps.

There is no external correlation between our reasons for jumping and the outcome of our landing, except for our response to change. For example, a positive reason may lead to a landing that "feels bad," and vice-versa. Therefore, the type of landing is determined by our perception of the jump and our response to change—all of which are based on our feelings, emotions, and judgments, and are heavily influenced by, among other things: our confidence, beliefs, hopes, courage, and past experiences. In this way, how we feel after landing is uniquely individual.

Whatever the type of landing, whether we feel good, bad, or in pain, the process remains the same. Thankfully, emotions and how we feel about things are usually temporary, with highs that turn into lows and lows that turn into highs. We may have good days where we feel on top of the world, followed by a bad day where we feel our world is crashing down on us.

The important thing is to be patient with ourselves, reminding ourselves that if jumping were easy, everyone would be doing it.

Have you experienced a major change in your life? Was it a result of a conscious decision you made, or something that "happened" to you? How did you handle the change? Did it turn out how you expected, planned, or hoped? Have you ever made a decision that you had expected would result in a happy outcome, but the reality was more difficult than you had expected? Are you aware of how your emotions affect your decision—and later, reaction—to change?

Ready for "getting over"?

Getting Over

After landing, the first thing we may face is our fears. One of the most inspiring quotes about overcoming fear, and one that has given me much encouragement during my own struggles, is from Nelson Mandela, also known as "Madiba" by his clan:

"I learned that courage was not the absence of fear, but the triumph over it. The brave man is not he who does not feel afraid, but he who conquers that fear."

In all of my struggles with courage, no matter when or under what circumstances, I have always blamed myself for having fear in the first place. In my life script that I replayed to myself, I deeply believed that being afraid was *bad*, that it was a sign of weakness. Survival was only guaranteed to the fittest: those who did not fear—the fearless. I have come to realize that growing up in the "ghetto," or what is now referred to today as the "hood," may have initially planted this idea.

And, this belief was further reinforced as I plotted my way through a lifetime of male-dominated fields of study and work: four years studying electricity in a vocational high school, three years studying electrical engineering in college (university), obtaining a Bachelor's degree in Finance (with hopes of working on Wall Street), working at Pfizer developing global IT systems', and later, as an established business owner advising members of the *Old Boys' Club* on their businesses. Growing up with addicts and under the threat of violence, and competing with men on their playing field for thirty years, led me to creating many unhealthy scripts about fears—to say the least.

When I first read the quote from Madiba—with tears in my eyes, sitting alone in my fair trade store—I knew he said it for people like me: those of us who have struggles and those of us who are afraid; in other words, *all of us.*

Those few, nicely-ordered words have profoundly changed the way I perceive fear and courage today, shattering a lifetime of reinforced scripts. I now believe that one does not exist without the other. It is only because we have fears that we are given the opportunity to have courage. And to have courage, we must overcome our fears.

This is the essence of "getting over."

Working their Way to the Surface

Overcoming our fears is largely dependent upon us first recognizing them. And, unlike jumping, which happens in the blink of an eye, identifying our fears after we have landed may take days, weeks, or even months. This is particularly the case when we have a deceptively high level of confidence and we are within our perceived comfort zone. It may take a number of situations for our fears to fully emerge. Here we must strike a delicate balance between maintaining confidence in ourselves, while being willing to accept outcomes other than the ones we had hoped, planned, or expected. It is our ability to consciously (and honestly) evaluate our situation that is critical to our success.

For example, six months after starting the business of your dreams, and being told that having an eighteen-month reserve of cash is enough to get you over the initial "hump"—the point at which the business begins making more than it spends—you begin to notice that your sales are much lower than expected. They are less than half of the amount that you anticipated at this point. You begin to realize that, at this rate, your reserves will not last the eighteen months that you predicted, but you still feel hopeful that sales will pick up. You tell yourself, *It is just a matter of time.*

Still certain that sales will increase, shortly after twelve months you begin making business purchases on your personal credit cards. After fifteen months in business, you are tired, exhausted, and have been working extra hours in order to save money on wages as you reach your credit cards' limits. Fearing your spouse's disapproval, you have been hiding the overdue bills and credit card statements, because you are ashamed and do not want your spouse to lose confidence in your ability to manage your business.

While you are well-educated, intelligent, clever, and thought this could never happen to you, the lack of money and constant exhaustion have brought up more fears than you ever imagined. Your fears have shaken the core of who you believed yourself to be. As a result, you begin to lose confidence in yourself and fall into despair. Whenever you are asked how business is going, it is always the same story: this order didn't arrive on time, or that equipment broke down. Or you blame someone else, your customers, other businesses, the local community, and the economy.

This example is a bit extreme, but it's a common occurrence for those taking the leap into business ownership. Often, it is easier to blame others, because we feel ashamed for failing, especially if we are in denial about the seriousness of the situation and fear other people's judgments about our abilities. It is easier to think, *This can't be happening to me, because I'm smart, educated, and clever,* than it is to take responsibility. The latter takes courage. By continuing to deny the truth of the situation, or believe that it can't be happening to us, sadly it is another self-placed obstacle in our path to overcoming our fears.

Two Faces of Fears: Lions and Tigers and Bears

Throughout my life, I've spent a lot of time thinking about fear. Perhaps it is because my mother has always feared for my life as a consequence of my surviving the failed abortion. During her pregnancy, she feared that I would be deformed or would be missing a limb.

Being raised in a dangerous neighborhood, she worried for my safety, always fearful the worst would happen. She always made me call home at "check-points" (years before mobile phones). I'd call before leaving a location and after arriving at a new location.

Surprisingly, calling my mother at check-points has carried well into my adult life, but now only when I travel. To be honest, there have been few days that I have not been in contact with my mother throughout my life. I do not fault her about this, even though I do put up a good verbal fight from time to time.

Now, as a mother myself, I cannot begin to imagine how the attempted abortion and my survival has impacted her.

Being more like my grandmother than my mother when it comes to how I approach life, death, and fear, and feeling that I've already escaped death once, I've taken a philosophical, pragmatic view, which is: *When it is my time to go, it will be my time. But until then, I will not live in fear.*

This is not to say that I do not have fears. I do—loads of them. Having grown up under the shadow of my mother's fears, believing that I wasn't supposed to be here, and therefore, shouldn't take life for granted, and having a strong dislike for feeling fearful, I've come up with several rational ways to help me find courage in the face of fear.

Recognizing that I am not a psychologist, nor have any formal psychology training, other than life itself, I am happy to share my view on fear. Again, take what works for you and leave what doesn't.

Earlier, I mentioned the concept of thinking of fear as my best friend, when I discussed my recent fear of driving in England. The "best friend" analogy is one I use for lighter, everyday fears—often situational in nature—like learning to drive, or accepting feedback from a boss during one of those dreaded annual performance evaluations.

For me, the best friend analogy has its own limitations and does not work when it comes to facing my deepest, darkest fears—the "ruin your life" type of fears.

For those fears, I have connected with my distant Native American roots and my experiences of living amongst Native Americans and mystical people for twenty years in New England, forming the basis for my own brand of blended spirituality. Taken from what is called "animal medicine," my homebrewed version is simply called, "lions and tigers and bears."

Putting external fears to one side, which includes an endless list of phobias, such as spiders or heights, there are two types of fears that affect our ability to make conscious decisions: internal and subconscious fears.

Internal fears are associated with low self-esteem and lack of confidence. They include fears of being: abandoned, unloved, rejected, unworthy, criticized, ridiculed, and a failure.

Subconscious fears are another type of internal fear, but are associated with our beliefs, such as shame and not feeling "good" enough. For example, when we feel we are not a good parent, a good wife, or a good person. To some extent, subconscious fears also include the fear of the unknown.

The basic premise behind lions and tigers and bears is that our fears have two faces: one that dazzles us with its magnificent beauty, leading us to not fear it; the other shows us what we are deathly scared of.

Lions and tigers and bears reminds me to keep a grounded perspective, allowing me to recognize the feeling of fear *and* admire the opportunity it presents.

For example, many people love to watch nature programs on television. My favorite was always the *Big Cat Diaries* on the Discovery Channel. Watching from a position of safety, at a distance through the screen of a television, it was easy to appreciate the majestic, regal, larger-than-life qualities of the female lioness, without any threat to my personal safety.

Of the few things I am certain of, I am absolutely certain that if I went out to my car at dusk and saw that same female lioness majestically walking down the street, as I have on numerous occasions with wild coyotes, I would be petrified—to put it mildly.

But that's exactly how the two faces of fear work. Up close and in person, these beautiful, wild animals may scare us to death, but from a position of safety, they do not pose a threat. As with our own fears, we may admire their inherent qualities, at times believing them to be an asset to us, while we unknowingly revel in them.

I seek to get as close as I can to my fears, not because I want to kill them but, instead, because I want to appreciate and understand what they are showing me about myself. By getting to know the animal (the fear), metaphorically, I may begin to appreciate, and later absorb, its traits, qualities, and characteristics—in other words, its animal medicine.

Unsuccessfully trying for many years to get rid of my fears, I have learned to accept them, even my deepest, darkest ones; rightly or wrongly, they make me who I am. Therefore, I no longer seek to kill my fears, any more than I would want to kill a female lioness.

Today, my idea of conquering a fear is to be at peace with it. Like all things in life, they too serve a purpose. I have no desire to live in fear, but to walk alongside it—as I would a majestic animal—then I may have the courage of a lion, the power of a tiger, and the strength of a bear.

Know that when we stand up and face our fears, we earn a golden opportunity to overcome them. Fears are our greatest source of internal power. Like lions, tigers, and bears, they too may give us courage, power, and strength!

Reflecting versus Regretting

Whether it is a mental jump, which causes us to make physical changes, or a physical jump, which results in a shift in our thinking, fundamentally, we must believe we have landed, give ourselves time and space to heal after landing, and seek ways to adapt to our new mental and physical realities, all while facing our fears.

While I have greatly oversimplified these steps, do not be fooled; this is where the hard work begins. Getting up and facing our fears, whether we feel good, bad, or in pain, provides us a golden ticket—not for a tour of a chocolate factory, but for a real chance to overcome our fears! Only then may we truly live with no regret.

In all jumps, there will be ups and downs; we will encounter old and new fears that will challenge us after we've landed, making it difficult to get up. It is then natural to have doubts, to question—or even reexamine—our decisions after going through the experience, and to live with both the positive and negative consequences of our actions.

Thinking about and reflecting on our experience with jumping may help us assess our situation, giving us insight on how to best adapt to our new reality. Thoughtfully asking ourselves, *"Did I make the right decision?"* may lead us to further examine our beliefs, expectations, and feelings.

If we feel that we made the wrong decision, we may then consider: What are the faults in my beliefs? What really makes my situation worse than before? Is it because my expectations have not been fulfilled, or my pride has been hurt? Why do I fear life not turning out how I want it to, or situations that compromise my confidence? How can I overcome these fears?

On the other hand, if we drift too far from these reflective thought-based activities into the negative, emotional side, it may give rise to us: blaming ourselves or others. We may also find ourselves teetering on the edge of regret. Or, if we landed far from where we were, we may become filled with despair, as I did after my last jump.

Should we find ourselves slipping down this negative, emotional-based spiral, it is a good indicator that we still have work to do. Perhaps we have not fully accepted responsibility for our decision on all levels—emotionally, mentally, physically, and spiritually—or we have not come to terms with accepting the consequences of our decision.

Further, we may not have fully committed ourselves to the belief that: we alone are solely responsible for our happiness. We may believe that someone or something else will make us happy. Personally, while I generally believe most people seek happiness after jumping, I usually seek to be at peace, then I know I have accepted the consequences of jumping.

The whole point of jumping is so that we will land with the greatest potential to walk away from our landing site and "get on" with our new life. We must diligently safeguard against becoming victims, by not allowing ourselves to be held back by our fears, regrets, and past failures. By consciously re-evaluating our beliefs, and letting go of judgments that keep us in the dark about the reality of our new situation, we may begin to recognize any new fears we encounter, and deal with them in a reflective, thought-provoking way.

If we have done this, we may get up, get over, and get on, walking away from our jump empowered—self-empowered.

Do you often think about, or reflect on, the decisions you've made? Have you thought about what you'd do differently if you had to make the same decision again? Are there decisions that you regret making? What causes you to feel regretful? Do you see an identifiable pattern when reflecting or regretting?

The Final Outcome (Part One):
Shattering Our Beliefs but Not Ourselves

Much has become clear to me as I near the end of writing this book: How I blamed myself and others; how easy I too fell into becoming a victim; and how my grandmother's wisdom helped me to rebuild trust and belief in myself, which has been my salvation.

After the move to England, I spent months blaming myself for my past business failures, which I believed was responsible for our financial struggles. I felt angry and resentful toward my husband for making the move more stressful than it had to be, because of his incessant financial worrying, which I believed was responsible for me giving up more than I had to (getting rid of my possessions to save on shipping, spending more on home repairs, reducing the home price) and a lot more than him. Having been self-employed for ten years, I had lost confidence in myself, felt old and out-of-touch with the modern workplace, and lacked the desire to re-climb the corporate latter, which I believed were the reasons I was unable to find a new job after moving.

I felt vulnerable, because I'd lost my financial independence, which I believed forced me to rely on my husband for everything—from finances to even the most basic things, such as: getting bank accounts, shopping for groceries, driving to interviews, deciding on purchases, and finding friends. Each time I asked my husband for money, a lifetime of pain stabbed me in the heart and generations of strong Irish women in my soul. However, the hardest pill to swallow was the feeling that I'd let my daughter down, because I'd forced her to give up everything in the States for a promise of a better life in England, and I had failed to make that happen.

These were my actual scripts. While they may appear overly simplified, they took many months, tears, and compassionately honest discussions with my husband to clearly articulate them.

But that is the point: the simpler we make our scripts, the easier it will be for us to clearly see the faults in our thinking. My scripts showed me that I did not believe myself to be the reason for my pain and suffering, but rather, something or someone else was always to blame, which was often my husband, because he was an undeserving, easy target. Additionally, even my confidence had failed me!

So when I heard my grandmother's voice in that early morning dream, commanding me to stop crying and open my eyes, I began to see how wrong I was. Not that the decision to move to England was the wrong decision (it was much deeper than that). It was my expectations and beliefs for life *after landing* that were wrong!

Prior to moving, I had developed a rigid set of expectations and beliefs on how life would be after we moved to England, and when they did not come to fruition, I refused to accept full responsibility. With—what I thought to be—realistic expectations in one hand, and a rigid set of beliefs in the other, I hit the ground running, so to speak. It was clear as a bell in my mind: I would find a well-paying job, like the one I had in the States; pay my daughter's university fees; and enjoy wonderful holidays with the UK's large vacation allowances. My vision was simple, clean, and realistic. I wasn't expecting to buy the moon.

I was, however, expecting a straightforward, peaceful life going into my mid-forties—like everyone else. I had a right to it—like everyone else. I deserved it—like everyone else—not because it was handed to me on a silver platter, but because I had worked damn hard for it. In my mind, I had earned it! I had a college degree from a good university, a boat load of desirable experience, and had worked twenty-five years for it.

But most unsettling of all, I deeply believed that it was owed to me for sacrificing so much to get to where I was: experiencing a lifetime of hard knocks and painful jumps I was forced to make, trading loved ones in a black world for a better life in a white world, struggling for years in business while unconsciously relinquishing my financial security to fight for the security of women in the developing world, and giving away most of my worldly possessions (which hurt more than expected, because I held a vestige of middle-class American entitlement, unknowingly absorbed by living in the entitled white world). In my mind, I had paid my pound of flesh.

So when I fell into a deep, fearful depression, and completely fell apart mentally and physically, racked with pain most of the time, unable to find a job, and therefore, unable to help my daughter financially or pay for her tuition, I lost all confidence in myself—it shattered me into a thousand pieces. I became unrecognizable to my loved ones and to myself. It was as if the last five years of stress and loss—that I refused to acknowledge or accept at the time—had caught up with me.

As I mentioned, it took months to clearly see and articulate my scripts. Once I had, and replayed them back to myself, I heard the pitiful, victimized *reasons* for my suffering, and saw the faults in my beliefs and expectations.

My scripts were telling me that nothing happened how I believed, expected, deserved, or hoped it would. In fact, the *exact opposite* occurred. Each painful wound was re-opened with each new job rejection or failed test. I was shocked by the depth in which I grieved over giving up my material possessions, as I did not consciously consider myself to be a materialistic person.

But in reality, none of that mattered. All that mattered was I had simply forgot that I was the only person responsible for my decisions and happiness, and further, my own peace of mind, *no matter the outcome.*

I will not lie; it took a hell of a lot of courage to wade through the emotional debris that I needed to get rid of in order to stop crying, and to face the pain-coated fears buried deep within my beliefs, before I was able to see my scripts clearly. It was not easy, to say the least. But when I did, like the times before, I emerged strong, confident, and self-empowered.

Unlike before, however, this time I had emerged with maturity, and a healthy dose of humility and compassion. I reckon this was due to the depth of my past despair, the physical pain I had endured, and one of the major benefits of being in one's forties: the acceptance of what is.

Only after I fully accepted the simple fact that I alone was responsible for my mind, body, and soul, I found the peace and happiness that I was responsible for making happen. What was done was done. It was what it was. And it was time for *getting on.*

Ready for "getting on"?

Getting On

For this last section of this book, I struggle to find the right words to adequately describe what I mean by "getting on." Perhaps this is because it is more challenging to define a feeling, rather than a situation or an event. In many ways, it is easier to describe how you know you've *gotten on*, than it is to define what it is meant by *getting on*.

So what is getting on? In a nutshell, and as its name implies, getting on occurs when we begin to fully enjoy our new, post-jump lives, usually indicated by two key factors. First, we have dealt with and overcome our fears—both our pre-jump and post-jump fears. Second, we have fully accepted responsibility for our decision to jump and the outcome after we landed.

I suspect it may sound too simple, too easy. But in reality, it rarely happens all at once, in every aspect of our lives, nor can we draw a line in the sand and say to ourselves, *From this day forward, I am getting on.* In my experience, it happens little by little, day by day, and in one area of our life at a time. That's why it is more beneficial to describe how you know you've gotten on.

A basic heartfelt way that we know that we're getting on, is when we find ourselves laughing or smiling, or simply feeling happy for no apparent reason. It may happen out of the blue, like when we look at a loved one and suddenly feel the love we had felt for them before the jump (this is especially true for loved ones who have passed on). For example, when we look up at the photo of our husband, wife, or partner on the wall in our home, instead of the usual hurt you felt each time you looked at the photo, your heart is now filled with love. Without your tearful eyes, you can, once again, see the twinkle in their eye.

Or, perhaps during lunch with co-workers, instead of the silent, seething anger you normally feel, from blaming yourself for leaving a perfectly good job because you wanted "more" out of life, you now find yourself laughing at your cube-mate's silly jokes. You never realized how funny they were!

These are some of the first clues that we are nearing the proverbial "light at the end of the tunnel," that we've made it through the worse part and now it is time to enjoy life again.

Conversely, we may find that we are *not* getting on when we are "tested." A situation will arise that allows us to see that we still have a script that needs to be reviewed, or a fear to overcome, or that we have yet to truly accept responsibility for our decisions and actions.

For example, you may think to yourself, or even say to others, that you have fully accepted your and your partner's decision not to have another child. But when your mother tells you that your younger sister is pregnant with her first child, you feel a stabbing pain in your heart. Since learning of her pregnancy, you find yourself avoiding her, you begin to internally blame your partner for forcing the decision on you, and you slowly begin to lose confidence in yourself. Once again, you begin to feel incomplete as a woman. Feelings and thoughts like these indicate that we still have work to do.

If, on the other hand, you are taken aback and saddened by the news and have a cry to clear the emotional debris that arose, the next day you visit your sister to share in her joy. When you see her, you are filled with happiness for her.

When the baby is born, the last vestiges of pain you may have felt are gone and are replaced with honest-to-goodness joy, because you have fully gotten on.

Have you ever experienced a major change that caused more pain than you believed you could bear, such as the death of a loved one, a life-altering health issue, or a severe change in financial security? Can you recall a time afterwards when you first found yourself happy, laughing, or smiling for no apparent reason? Did you feel guilty for feeling good, or did you feel a sense of relief? What did you notice was different after you allowed yourself to experience joy again?

Finding Purpose After Jumping

Of all the benefits we may experience after jumping, none are more profound, and potentially life-changing, than the emergence of our new stronger, more confident selves. Our journey from the cliff's edge to our new post-jump lives may have required us to change tremendously, not only our physical environment, but emotionally, mentally, and spiritually. This transformation, from living in fear to blossoming into our new lives, is symbolic of the lotus plant's journey from seed to flower.

Beginning its journey on the bed of a muddy pond, the lotus plant grows a long root until it rises above the murky water. When it reaches the surface of the water and faces the sun, the leaves of the lotus flower will open, revealing its beautifully clean petals, untouched by the mud from which it came. Each night it tightly closes its delicate petals and sinks below the surface of the murky water, protecting them throughout the night. The next day it blossoms again with the rising sun.

Similar to the lotus flower's journey from the muddy pond bed, through the murky water, and finally to the surface, where it blossoms under the sun's rays, accompanying the emergence of our new stronger selves, we too may begin to notice an awareness that we had not known before. Having overcome our fears, and having gotten on, we will emerge stronger, more confident, and with a greater self-belief.

When we take the time to reflect on the circumstances that initially led us to the cliff's edge and our journey over the cliff—having confidence and belief in ourselves; finding hope and courage to face our deepest, darkest fears; overcoming fears that may have held us back in the past; making the decision to jump; feeling the exhilaration and release as we go over the cliff; and lastly, discovering the inner strength to get up, get over, and get on—we may be amazed at what we have accomplished. We may began to realize how truly powerful we are.

This new awareness of ourselves may also lead us to question other aspects of our lives: our actions, ideas, motivations, thoughts, relationships, and so on. From our new position of self-empowerment, we may delve deeper to consider other aspects of our lives by reevaluating what matters most to us, determining the significance of our lives, understanding the impact our actions have on others, and discovering our purpose. After progressing through each phase of jumping (preparing, jumping, and landing), and having fully gotten on, we will find that opportunities begin to open up for us that were not there before. For me, by jumping off the "no more babies" cliff that I described earlier, I began a journey of self-discovery, where I began to question my life's purpose. Several years later, and with much support and encouragement from my husband and daughter, I jumped again—into a life filled with purpose.

Following in the spirit of my grandmother's footsteps, who helped to free me from the shackles of poverty, I, in turn, created opportunities for other women through fair trade. With other pioneering fair traders, we enabled women in developing countries to become financially independent and provided them with the resources to care for their children.

Working in the fair trade movement also allowed me to lovingly nurture the part of me that wanted, once again, to feel the joys of birth, while at the same time, filling me with a sense of purpose, by helping other women and their children.

When we take a moment to celebrate our accomplishments and our newfound selves after getting on—in other words, "have our day in the sun"—we may experience one of life's most treasured gifts blossoming before our eyes: a world of possibility.

The Final Outcome (Part Two): The Stillness of Getting On

When I initially outlined the structure of this book, being a logically-driven person, it all seemed so clear: the process, the steps, and the outcomes. Despite offering much advice within these pages about not setting expectations, and further, having learned that it was my expectations that needed to be shattered for me to build a new life, I still find myself expecting outcomes.

I felt in my heart that I was getting on—I was smiling, laughing, and loving again. I fully accepted my decision and responsibility for my actions since jumping. I was no longer filled with anger, resentment, or fighting "what is," but doing my best to embrace change.

I also re-tuned my hearing, and no longer had to read lips to understand the different uses of words and strange accents. I adjusted my diet, exercise, and supplements to deal with my continued health issues in the new environment. I re-learned how to dress, and bought more suitable clothes for the damp, windy, and cool weather, so that I didn't freeze, or itch, all the time—dressing in many layers, and avoiding woolly jumpers. I re-wired my brain to look right, then left; drive on the left side of the road; and learned how to master roundabouts!

I let go of my pride and asked for help, and sought lesser-paying jobs. With each job rejection, whether it was because of my residency status, or lack of "local" experience, I no longer let it destroy the confidence I'd built. And lastly, I openly and honestly accepted my husband's financial support, even learning to find humor in my newly dependent life, and in my "homemaker salary", which enabled me to obtain my first credit card in England.

But in spite of doing what I could to get on—meaning, anything within my control—I still was not moving forward. While my daughter held down two jobs, I had yet to find one job, let alone become financially stable again, nor had I even earned one single sterling pound after twelve months.

I had yet to make close friends of my own, excluding those who weren't already my husband's friends before we moved here (whom I absolutely love!). I was still in pain most of the time, suffering from bouts of memory lapses, inflammation, and exhaustion.

Furthermore, I had failed both my financial exam and my driving test (twice on the latter). While I expected to fail the financial exam, unfortunately, I did not expect to fail the driving test. The first time I failed, I triumphantly shed only a few tears, and never once hit the stomach-curdling cry of total despair. The second time I failed, I screamed and shouted with anger and lots of expletives.

After failing the driving test the first time, my husband consoled me and was happy to hear that I'd planned to take the test again right away. I texted my daughter, who responded in utter disbelief, of course, with hands-to-face emojis.

Then I called my mother, only to listen to her lengthy monologue about the first time I'd failed something. It was a chemistry class, during my first year at college, studying electrical engineering. I kept up with my assignments, studied, and worked extensively with tutors. Prior to receiving my first failing grade, I had never failed at anything—*ever*. So each time I received a failing exam, I would call my mother and grandmother, crying, sometimes even vomiting. My grandmother was more matter-of-fact, much like my husband. But my mother usually just listened to me cry, mostly speechless, or offered an occasional, "Oh Mar, I'm so sorry."

She told me for the first time recently that she never knew what to say to me when I called crying. Not because she didn't love me, but because she never had the confidence that I had. She simply couldn't understand what it felt like to fail at something when you expected *not* to fail. She always expected to fail.

I didn't know whether to cry *for* my mother, or *because* of my mother's words, as it was her genius that helped me to find the final resolution—the last "ah-ha"—for this book. Her words helped me to see clearly that what I thought were failures—job rejections, failed tests, and lack of financial independence—were part of my lessons to learn from my last jump. Unknowingly, her words were the Balm of Gilead that I sought to heal these freshly made wounds from yet another perceived "failure."

Herein lies the last golden nugget of this book: Getting on does *not* mean moving on. Getting on is a state of mind, and is solely within our control. On the other hand, *moving on* is a change in our physical reality, and is *not*, in the tiniest bit, in our control. Getting on is that momentary stillness that gives us the opportunity, like the lotus flower, to blossom under the sun's rays.

Allowing ourselves this momentary stillness to revel in our newly found self-empowerment, we fully incorporate the lessons we have learned from the jump, and this enables us to clearly see the possibilities that exist for moving on.

If we move on to the next path, opportunity, job, task, situation, and have not found the stillness from the last jump—that is, we have not recognized our own strength, confidence, and self-belief—then we risk losing it. It is similar to winning a game, then moving on to the next game before collecting the prize from the first game. Ultimately, we risk becoming a victim, because we have not fully garnered the self-empowerment that our jump has afforded us.

Ultimately, getting on means: "I am at peace and fully accept what is, at this moment in time."

Getting on, to me, says: "Pass or fail, win or lose, get the job or don't get the job, I am happy with my new life and my decision to jump." Getting on, to me, says: "Thank you to my husband, for his love, support, and eternal patience, with all my heart," without any leftover feelings of anger or resentment. Getting on, to me, says: "I can say that I am truly proud of all that my daughter has achieved," without any pangs of guilt or feeling that I'm a bad mother for forcing her to grow up too fast; making her work for her own money; uprooting her from her cushy, middle-class life; and selling all of our possessions. Getting on, to me, says: "I'm sorry, Mom, for moving so far away…" without the usual feelings of guilt and responsibility. "…I love you with all my heart and hope that, one day, you will find peace and happiness, in spite of your constant pain."

Lastly, getting on, to me, says: "Thank you, Grandma Rita, for your healing words, all those years ago, for without them, I could not have stood up, overcome my fears, and got on with my new life. I will always miss you, and I now understand the sacrifices that you made for us. I know that it is because of your love and support that I can once more experience the deepest joy and love for living again."

I imagined that once I finished this book, my life would be all sorted—I'd have a well-paid job, money in the bank, and would be feeling healthy again. I hoped to fill these last pages with an amazing happily-ever-after ending. But I'm sorry to disappoint, as this is not the case. I suppose it's a more realistic—dare I say—British ending, rather than a Hollywood, Disney-style ending.

The truth of the matter is, I do not know what tomorrow will bring, or what opportunities lie ahead. To quote my grandmother, I do not know if tomorrow will bring "another day and another dollar," or if I will be pain-free, with my health fully restored.

But I do know one thing for certain: I will be ready for whatever life does bring.

With love,

Marcie

1979 Busch Gardens, Florida

AFTERWORD

But I do know one thing for certain: I will be ready for whatever life brings.

It has been almost a year since I wrote that last sentence, when I finished "writing" the book in early-September 2014, one year after moving to England. In retrospect, it now seems as though I tempted fate by setting those words so boldly in print. I am now inclined to think that, perhaps the written word is heard more loudly by those in charge of our fate, thus ensuring a rapid response.

Did I really, truly believe I would be ready for whatever life would bring? How naive I was to think that I was ready and still, in some small way, continue to be.

Six days after launching the book, I found myself wailing like a baby, falling over—unable to stand, my legs buckling from the invisible weight of metaphorically balancing my mother's life in my hands—repeating over and over to family, friends, doctors, and myself: "I'm not ready for this. I'm not ready for this. Oh God, I'm *really* not ready for this." I could not help but think to myself: *Why had I written those damn words? I'm not ready for this!*

But first, let me regress to the events that happened after writing those last words…

About a month after I finished writing this book, it seemed as though someone had flipped a new "life switch," because many exciting and challenging events began to transpire. The first of which was finding an editor to help me polish the book for publishing. After our initial consultation, she gave me the first of several deadlines: I had one month to send her my book for editing.

While I was hoping to get my book professionally edited sooner, the time gave me the opportunity to do what many had been suggesting to me: take a break from editing. This advice, at first, seemed counterproductive, as I wanted to spend the time continuing to pour over every word of my manuscript.

After a two-week break from editing, however, I had gained a fresh perspective and deepened my understanding of the concepts I had written about. In the end, I was grateful that I'd had the extra time.

I also interviewed and was accepted for a board of trustees' seat on a charity dedicated to mentoring young entrepreneurs. This was especially momentous for me, as I had been volunteering for the charity for some time, and I looked forward to the challenges of the new role. I especially felt a sense of achievement because I was one of the first trustees who lacked an aristocratic title or community honor, and those who have them are referred to as "the great and the good."

Lastly, I received an invitation to interview for a contract job at my daughter's university preparing research grant applications. While I looked forward to the upcoming interview, I fought hard to quell my expectations for getting the job, in order to avoid disappointment if I wasn't chosen for the position.

Before the date of the interview, my husband and I went on vacation in Cyprus, to celebrate our one-year anniversary of our move to England.

When we returned from Cyprus, my quiet garden, market, and pub-strolling life had ended. I went to the interview, but I was not selected for the job. However, unlike previous rejections, I was recommended for another position at the university. This one had project management responsibilities, similar to my previous work at Pfizer and as a retail business owner. In other words, the job was highly demanding, generally stressful, and had tight deadlines.

I was asked to start the new job in three days, which was the same week I was scheduled to send my book to the editor! To complicate matters, the job was two hours from my home, so daily commuting was not an option. However, I was up for the challenge, so I nervously accepted the position in late-October.

After working the first day of my first job in a new country, my husband and I found a quiet room for me in a private Airbnb home.

Our vacation to Cyprus now seemed to be a distant memory. It was hard to imagine that, just two weeks prior, I had been leisurely lounging by the side of a pool, enjoying a welcomed break from a year-long job search. And now I found myself working in a large, one-room office with twelve strangers during the day, living with four strangers at night, and returning home by train every weekend with my bright, blue-trimmed suitcase in hand.

I had long planned to visit my mom in the States for Christmas vacation. But because of a respiratory emergency she had had before Thanksgiving, I changed the focus of my visit by reducing planned visits with friends in order to spend more time with her.

The night before my flight, I spent a lovely evening with my husband at a hotel near Heathrow Airport, where we exchanged small gifts and transferred my clothes from my workweek suitcase to my larger travel suitcase. The next morning, I flew to the States—for the first time since moving to England—to visit my mom.

When I arrived, I discovered that my mom was now smoking significantly less, getting physical therapy to strengthen her breathing, and receiving more home care, which she had long needed because of her pain but had previously been denied. These positive changes put my mind at ease, and it was comforting to know that she was now being properly taken care of.

Having received the suggested changes to the book from my editor before going to the States, and because of my jet lag, I worked on the second draft of my book in the pre-dawn hours. The afternoons I saved for working on house jobs: cleaning, cooking, straightening, washing linens, and scrubbing tobacco-stained walls. I bought my mom a new computer and helped her to get on Facebook and to set up her email.

My mom and I had a difficult time at first, because of all the changes I was "forcing" on her—by decluttering her house and overwhelming her with the new technology. But, I knew our time together was very limited, so I tried to do as much as I could for her.

Thankfully, the visit with my mom ended nicely, where my mom, my step-father, and I met up with my daughter—who was already in the States—a few days before our flights back to England. My parents were happy to visit with my daughter, as it had been over a year since we'd all spent time together. They were also thrilled about their first stay in a dog-friendly hotel. Each morning, my mom and her dog sped side-by-side down the long, wide corridor to breakfast, breaking in her Christmas present: a flashy, red scooter with a wire basket. We all took turns riding the scooter and trying out the various speeds—identified by turtle and hare symbols.

Returning from the States, I had a few days at home to celebrate the New Year with my husband, and then I went back to work, and back to my workweek suitcase.

Being driven by the idea that my writing would potentially give me the financial freedom to travel with my husband and have frequent visits with my mom, over the next three months I ferociously worked on finalizing my book and setting up a publishing business: completing several rounds of edits with my editor, obtaining ISBNs, creating a brand identity, designing a website and a book cover, deciding on distributors, and getting blurbs and bios written.

To reduce my daily commute to work, I moved out of the Airbnb rented room and into a stylish, French bed and breakfast (B&B) in a gritty part of town, amongst ethnic restaurants, drag venues, and gay adult toy shops. I could now walk to work, and had more time to spend with new friends and family. My husband began staying with me at the B&B once a week, where we indulged ourselves by pretending to be on holiday and exploring new cuisines.

With a work contract extension and the possibility of more work in the future, my husband and I felt secure enough to rent a small *bungalow*—a ranch-style home near my job that would allow us to spend more time together. The rented home also gave me hope that my mother would be able to visit us over the summer, because it did not have stairs like our permanent home. For the first time since moving to England, I felt excited about the future and connected to my new home country.

It had been a long seven months—filled with many twists and turns—since I wrote the last words in the book, but the finish line—publication of the book—was now in sight.

There were many times when fear would completely overtake me—fear of telling my and my family's secrets and of being ridiculed about my writing—causing me to have nightmares or awake in the middle of the night in a panicky sweat. But thanks to reassurance from loved ones, especially my mom, and my editor, I was able to overcome my anxiety.

In the beginning of March, with a final manuscript in hand, I focused on preparing an official book launch for my Grandmother Rita's birthday: April 19th. I first double-checked with my family to make sure they were ready for me to tell our story.

While I had gotten my mom's "permission" before I started writing, and read many sections of the book to her as I wrote them, I emailed her a copy of the finished manuscript so that she could read it on her new laptop before the launch. She was understandably nervous about sharing our story, but she too felt a sense of relief, mostly from the lifting of the secret we had both carried: her abortion attempt when she was pregnant with me.

I called my uncle and told him about the book, as I had no greater claim over my grandmother than him. During my visit to the States, I'd spoken with my step-father, my "father," and my paternal grandmother. All had encouraged me to write the book.

For the next month, I made final preparations for launching the book as planned. I worked with my editor to convert the final manuscript into various electronic files for publishing. Once complete, I began uploading the files to a long list of US and UK distributor websites. With the help of my amazing graphic designer, I completed my website (which I dedicated to my mom); set up a blog and social media pages; and finalized the book cover. I settled on a tagline for my website that best fits the overall theme of my writing: "Marcie L Boyer on love, loss and the courage to live."

On Sunday, April 19th, I posted a note on Facebook as a "soft" launch of the book, and received an outpour of positive encouragement from friends and family. Based on the Amazon Sales Report, I sold two copies of the book within the first 24 hours: the first to a buyer in the UK (who my husband insisted wasn't him), and the other to a buyer in the US (which my mom happily told me was her, with the help of her aide). Overcome with excitement, I decided to wait until the following weekend to launch my social media pages.

Friday afternoon, April 24th, I worked from home in order to meet a tight work deadline. My mom and I talked briefly around her lunch time (my dinner time), as we did most days. She said she couldn't talk for too long because her aide would be arriving soon and she wanted to shower first. We talked for about 20 minutes, then we started to say our usual

"I love you" goodbyes, but the tone was slightly different—more casually thoughtful.

She started with her usual, "I love you, Mar."

I quickly replied in my normal manner, "I love you too, Ma."

But instead of our quick, it's-time-to-hang-up goodbyes, she hesitated, then slowly responded with, "I really do love you, Mar."

Sensing the change in her tone, I said, "I know you do, Ma, and you know I love you too."

To that she responded, "I'm so proud of you. A mother could not have asked for a better daughter."

Then we said goodbye.

Those were my mother's last spoken words to me.

The next three days I have stored away in a dream-like time capsule in my mind, ring-fenced from real life, and consisting of surreal flash-backs.

The next day—Saturday afternoon—I hurriedly dashed out for a walk—before the rain—to the sheep paddock at the castle down the hill from our home, to see how much the "babies" (lambs) had grown from the week before. I also went grocery shopping.

Then I called my mom, at our usual time, while making a homemade pizza, but I got no answer. I left a message, assuming she and my step-father were out shopping and she'd call me back when they returned.

After dinner, I received a series of texts from my step-father, telling me to call his cell phone. When I called him back, he spoke slowly, but it did not matter—his words were lost on me, because my mind would not accept them; those that escaped felt like daggers piercing through my heart, "…unconscious…floor…lost too much blood…no brain activity…" I handed the phone to my husband as my legs gave way with my step-father's last three words: "…making her comfortable."

The next day—Sunday afternoon—I arrived at the hospital where my mother was being cared for (which was also the hospital I had been born in—the one my mother believed the angels had visited when they'd blessed me with life, because of her failed abortion). This arrival followed a 24-hour, 3,000-mile journey across the Atlantic, with several "close calls" that involved cell phone calls to my step-father from the terminal, runway, and baggage claim, asking him to plead to the doctors to do whatever they could to keep my mother alive until my daughter and I got there.

For the first time, I realized: it wasn't *me* the angels had blessed at my birth—it was *my mother*. For it was *her* dream they had made come true on the day of my birth; it was *her* prayers that had been answered—by giving me a healthy, normal life, despite the abortion procedure.

As I stepped out of my mother's car on the hospital grounds, I looked up to the sky and realized that this was the day they had blessed *me*, by making it possible for us to get there before they took her from me. I thanked the angels as I walked through the double doors.

The next 24 hours was all the time I had to make a lifetime of decisions, some of which felt so heavy that my legs, at times, could not support me. Thankfully, I did not have to make the decisions alone, as I had a tribe of love and support from my family. Through tears and pain, we had to decide: *How long would we keep her on life support? Would we donate her organs? Who needed to say goodbye to her?*

Privately, I struggled with heartbreakingly impossible questions that tested the bond of mother and daughter: *How would I, her only daughter, know when she was ready to be let go? Would I have the strength to let her go, my mother—the person who loves me unconditionally and taught me to love the same way? How would I say goodbye? How would it affect my daughter?*

Early Monday morning, I spent four pre-dawn hours alone with my mother. For the first time since arriving at the hospital, my mother's room was quiet. I took her hand, kissed her cheek, and brushed the wispy "baby" hairs from her forehead. Her eyes were softly shut, and the folds of her face were soft—no longer carrying the pain she suffered each and every day. She looked peaceful—for the first time in many, many years. I played her favorite Karen Carpenter songs and reminded her about happy times and the love we shared.

I also told her about the new realization I'd had about the angels—that they had seen the strength of her love for me and they had blessed her, not me, the day I was born. I told her that I had thanked them for making it possible for me to say goodbye to her. I cried the heaviest tears, and then we both slept.

On Monday afternoon, it was clear to all that my mother was ready. I collected myself, and focused my thoughts on my daughter: *Was she ready to say goodbye to her grandmother? Was she ready to walk through this door, as I had done 22 years earlier when my Grandmother Rita passed away?*

I asked my daughter if she wanted to stay with me for her grandmother's passing, or if she would rather stay with the tribe of family in the special waiting room the hospital provided for these precious final moments. I explained to her that, unlike ordinary doors, this particular door could not be returned through once entered—it would shut forever, and she would never view life the same way again. I told her it was a "sacred door," because it was a privilege and an honor to help our loved ones to pass.

This time, I was ready—unlike the 23-year-old newlywed I had been when my grandmother passed away. My daughter said she wanted to be there—for me.

With my mother wrapped like a baby in my arm in front of me, my heart to her heart, my daughter behind me, holding me up, hand-in-hand with the rest of our immediate family who surrounded the bed, all offering their words of love, I whispered into my mother's ear, my last words to her: "I love you, Ma, I really do. Be free…go be free."

Finding Purpose: The Reason for it all

When I started writing this book over a year ago, my move to England—my last major jump—was the focal point of my ideas, along with the accompanying challenges I'd faced with moving. My intention for writing the book—wanting to share my experiences and insight with others who are going through similar, difficult times—has not changed, neither have the principles that are involved with making major life changes: listening to our inner voice, finding the courage to make difficult decisions, making difficult decisions despite what others think, taking responsibility for the outcome of our jumps, developing patience with ourselves, becoming open to self-discovery, and finding purpose after a major life change.

But what *has* changed since my mother passed is how I view the *purpose* of this book. While the move to England—and the ensuing challenges—has shattered many expectations I had once held—and continues to affect my day-to-day life— I realize now that moving to another country was *not* the most important challenge I had faced, nor do I believe it was the underlining purpose for writing this book.

Retrospectively, I now see the role the book has played in preparing me for the greatest challenge I would face: the death of my mother. Therefore, the true purpose for writing this book was to prepare me for finding the courage to fulfill a lifelong promise to my mother: to be there for her—always. To achieve that momentous feat, it took every fiber of my being.

And I believe this newly discovered purpose was the reason for it all: hearing my grandmother's dream-like voice telling me to open my eyes, and seeing the gifts she had given me all those years ago; making the decision to write this book, to heal from my last jump; talking with my mother throughout the year on each topic in the book, helping both of us heal from a lifetime of guilt and shame; and even examining and researching the process of making difficult decisions for the content of this book.

It is clear to me that the move to England played a significant part, by creating a path for my mother and me to heal. We talked more about life in our hour-long, daily phone conversations than we ever had. The newfound geographical distance between us birthed a need for our conversations—mostly as a result of our time differences and having less opportunity to talk.

Before moving, my mother and I usually spoke several times a day, in between our daily responsibilities, about insignificant topics. After moving, we had to *plan* our conversations, and with planning—and without the luxury of time—our talks became more valuable—precious.

From my perspective, I had to "budget" our conversation time by squeezing everything in, so that I could also share with her the things I was writing about in the book. This led to our awareness of the finality of the written word: we no longer had the luxury of having unanswered questions and lingering ideas; instead, we sought resolve—for past and present events and hurts—before they would be put into print.

Every word, every example, and every tear shed during the writing of this book, gave me the courage to make the two most painful decisions of my life, which culminated in a 48-hour period: to keep my mother alive so my daughter and I could be there for her last moments, and to withdraw my mother's life support so that she could go in peace.

My mother's death is now my latest jump, and the purpose for writing this book. I can now see how both my grandmother and my mother helped to prepare me for what I would face during their deaths, and how both have left a legacy of courage and love for me to follow.

I hesitate now to write these final last words, as I no longer wish to tempt fate. But because all books must have last words, here goes…

If I asked myself today, *Do I believe I am ready for whatever life brings?*, unlike my previous last words, my answer this time would not seek to be bold, clever, or courageous.

My answer would simply be: I hope that I am.

Love and blessings,

Marcie

Me and my mom, 1974.

Sandra Lee Boyer (1953 – 2015)

ACKNOWLEDGEMENTS

Firstly, I'd like to acknowledge and thank the two most amazing people in my life, my husband and daughter, for sharing their life, love, and adventures with me. I know it has been a long, arduous journey over the cliff for all of us. I love you both *muches*. Secondly, I'd like to thank my step-children and their families for their open arms these past seventeen years, and after our landing. No words can adequately express how much it has meant to have a loving tribe to welcome us to our new home country.

I am eternally grateful to: my mother, for her love, support, and encouragement, which enabled me to tell this story; my step-father, for his solid, reliable, tall shoulders, and never-ending help through each jump; both of them, for always giving the little they had so that my daughter and I always had what we needed; my "father," for his Southern Mississippian strength, teaching me not just to survive, but to thrive in the face of adversity; and my ex-husband, for his understanding and friendship through all my major jumps, his help with raising our daughter, and his continued help with designing the website and cover for this book.

I'd also like to thank: my soul-sister and poet, Rhonda Ward, for, after fifteen years, still surprising me with her insightful views on telling me how it is; and Karen C.L. Anderson, for encouraging me to write my story during our many chats in my fair trade store, and for providing her thoughtful foreword; and Christine Rice, for her professional editorial services, and for her sound advice and words of encouragement, which helped me to stay the course through the process of publishing this book.

For the enduring and new friendships along the path to the cliff's edge and landing as an immigrant in a foreign land, I'd like to enthusiastically thank: Deb Donovan and Peg Stroup, for moral support, and their words of encouragement to jump; Tracee Reiser and Tricia McAvoy, for providing examples of living life firm in purpose, and being strong female role models; Nick and Kay Atkins, for healing the soul with gut-wrenching laughter, gourmet home-cooked meals, and many glasses of wine after landing, and bringing glimmers of light to all they shine upon; and Hella Pierce and Anne Peace, for their compassionate and loving friendships; I'm also grateful to: Dr. Marianne Ford, for her patience each time that I fell to pieces in her exam room; Helen Shanks, for putting me back together again with her expert osteopathic hands; Jane at the Fitness Connection, for keeping my muscles long and strong with her sensitive teaching of Pilates; Jane at the bank, for helping me to get my financial footing; and Jane, Margaret, and Michelle, for their welcoming nature through their businesses that bring joy and happiness to our village.

Last, but not least, I'd like to thank the School Office staff, for providing me the opportunity to belong after landing, and for their heart-felt friendships.

Made in the USA
Charleston, SC
05 November 2015